Maintenance Of Software
Complete Self-Assessment Guide

The guidance in this Self-Assessment is based on Maintenance Of Software best practices and standards in business process architecture, design and quality management. The guidance is also based on the professional judgment of the individual collaborators listed in the Acknowledgments.

Table of Contents

About The Art of Service

The Art of Service, Business Process Architects since 2000, is dedicated to helping stakeholders achieve excellence.

Defining, designing, creating, and implementing a process to solve a stakeholders challenge or meet an objective is the most valuable role… In EVERY group, company, organization and department.

Unless you're talking a one-time, single-use project, there should be a process. Whether that process is managed and implemented by humans, AI, or a combination of the two, it needs to be designed by someone with a complex enough perspective to ask the right questions.

Someone capable of asking the right questions and step back and say, 'What are we really trying to accomplish here? And is there a different way to look at it?'

With The Art of Service's Standard Requirements Self-Assessments, we empower people who can do just that — whether their title is marketer, entrepreneur, manager, salesperson, consultant, Business Process Manager, executive assistant, IT Manager, CIO etc... —they are the people who rule the future. They are people who watch the process as it happens, and ask the right questions to make the process work better.

Contact us when you need any support with this Self-Assessment and any help with templates, blue-prints and examples of standard documents you might need:

http://theartofservice.com
service@theartofservice.com

Included Resources - how to access

Included with your purchase of the book is the Maintenance

Of Software Self-Assessment Spreadsheet Dashboard which contains all questions and Self-Assessment areas and auto-generates insights, graphs, and project RACI planning - all with examples to get you started right away.

How? Simply send an email to
access@theartofservice.com
with this books' title in the subject to get the Maintenance Of Software Self Assessment Tool right away.

You will receive the following contents with New and Updated specific criteria:

- The latest quick edition of the book in PDF

- The latest complete edition of the book in PDF, which criteria correspond to the criteria in...

- The Self-Assessment Excel Dashboard, and...

- Example pre-filled Self-Assessment Excel Dashboard to get familiar with results generation

- In-depth specific Checklists covering the topic

- Project management checklists and templates to assist with implementation

INCLUDES LIFETIME SELF ASSESSMENT UPDATES

Every self assessment comes with Lifetime Updates and Lifetime Free Updated Books. Lifetime Updates is an industry-first feature which allows you to receive verified self assessment updates, ensuring you always have the most accurate information at your fingertips.

Get it now- you will be glad you did - do it now, before you forget.

Send an email to **access@theartofservice.com** with this books' title in the subject to get the Maintenance Of Software Self Assessment Tool right away.

Purpose of this Self-Assessment

This Self-Assessment has been developed to improve understanding of the requirements and elements of Maintenance Of Software, based on best practices and standards in business process architecture, design and quality management.

It is designed to allow for a rapid Self-Assessment to determine how closely existing management practices and procedures correspond to the elements of the Self-Assessment.

The criteria of requirements and elements of Maintenance Of Software have been rephrased in the format of a Self-Assessment questionnaire, with a seven-criterion scoring system, as explained in this document.

In this format, even with limited background knowledge of Maintenance Of Software, a manager can quickly review existing operations to determine how they measure up to the standards. This in turn can serve as the starting point of a 'gap analysis' to identify management tools or system elements that might usefully be implemented in the organization to help improve overall performance.

How to use the Self-Assessment

On the following pages are a series of questions to identify to what extent your Maintenance Of Software initiative is complete in comparison to the requirements set in standards.

To facilitate answering the questions, there is a space in front of each question to enter a score on a scale of '1' to '5'.

1 Strongly Disagree

2 Disagree

3 Neutral

4 Agree

5 Strongly Agree

Read the question and rate it with the following in front of mind:

'In my belief, the answer to this question is clearly defined'.

There are two ways in which you can choose to interpret this statement;
1. how aware are you that the answer to the question is clearly defined
2. for more in-depth analysis you can choose to gather evidence and confirm the answer to the question. This obviously will take more time, most Self-Assessment users opt for the first way to interpret the question and dig deeper later on based on the outcome of the overall Self-Assessment.

A score of '1' would mean that the answer is not clear at all, where a '5' would mean the answer is crystal clear and defined. Leave emtpy when the question is not applicable or you don't want to answer it, you can skip it without affecting your score. Write your score in the space provided.

After you have responded to all the appropriate statements in each section, compute your average score for that section, using the formula provided, and round to the nearest tenth. Then transfer to the corresponding spoke in the Maintenance Of Software Scorecard on the second next page of the Self-Assessment.

Your completed Maintenance Of Software Scorecard will give you a clear presentation of which Maintenance Of Software areas need attention.

Maintenance Of Software
Scorecard Example

Example of how the finalized Scorecard can look like:

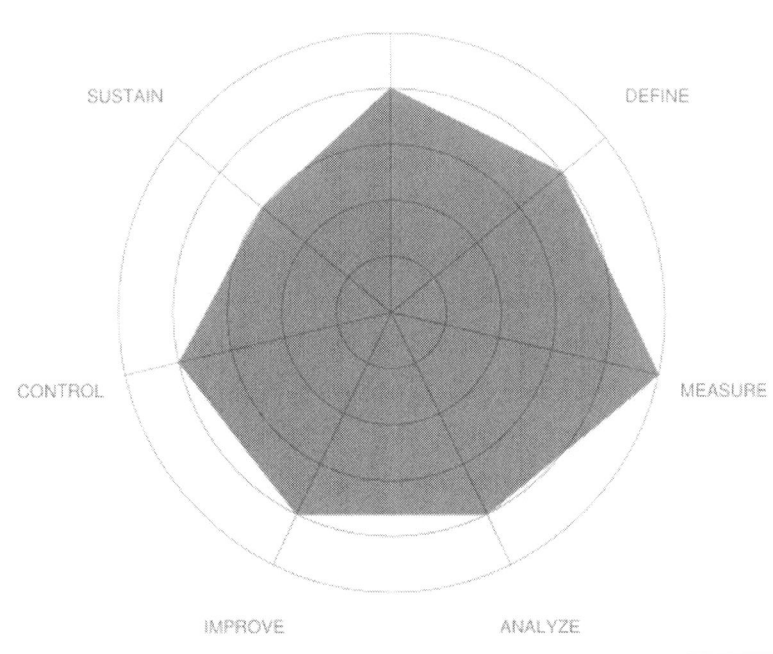

Maintenance Of Software Scorecard

Your Scores:

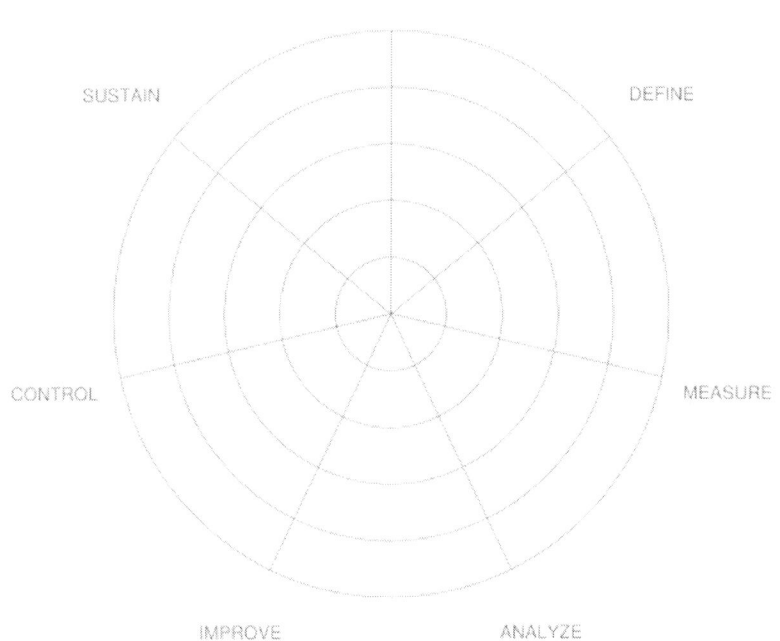

BEGINNING OF THE SELF-ASSESSMENT:

CRITERION #1: RECOGNIZE

INTENT: Be aware of the need for change. Recognize that there is an unfavorable variation, problem or symptom.

In my belief, the answer to this question is clearly defined:

5 Strongly Agree

4 Agree

3 Neutral

2 Disagree

1 Strongly Disagree

1. Does the problem have ethical dimensions?
<--- Score

2. To what extent does each concerned units management team recognize Maintenance of software as an effective investment?
<--- Score

3. What activities does the governance board need to

consider?
<--- Score

4. Would you recognize a threat from the inside?
<--- Score

5. Who are your key stakeholders who need to sign off?
<--- Score

6. What Maintenance of software problem should be solved?
<--- Score

7. What would happen if Maintenance of software weren't done?
<--- Score

8. How do you recognize an objection?
<--- Score

9. What Maintenance of software coordination do you need?
<--- Score

10. How are you going to measure success?
<--- Score

11. Who else hopes to benefit from it?
<--- Score

12. Are employees recognized or rewarded for performance that demonstrates the highest levels of integrity?
<--- Score

13. What vendors make products that address the Maintenance of software needs?
<--- Score

14. Do you need different information or graphics?
<--- Score

15. When a Maintenance of software manager recognizes a problem, what options are available?
<--- Score

16. Will a response program recognize when a crisis occurs and provide some level of response?
<--- Score

17. Where do you need to exercise leadership?
<--- Score

18. What extra resources will you need?
<--- Score

19. Are problem definition and motivation clearly presented?
<--- Score

20. Why the need?
<--- Score

21. Are there Maintenance of software problems defined?
<--- Score

22. What training and capacity building actions are needed to implement proposed reforms?
<--- Score

23. Is it needed?
<--- Score

24. Do you know what you need to know about Maintenance of software?
<--- Score

25. How do you assess your Maintenance of software workforce capability and capacity needs, including skills, competencies, and staffing levels?
<--- Score

26. What creative shifts do you need to take?
<--- Score

27. Will it solve real problems?
<--- Score

28. What situation(s) led to this Maintenance of software Self Assessment?
<--- Score

29. What does Maintenance of software success mean to the stakeholders?
<--- Score

30. What needs to stay?
<--- Score

31. What problems are you facing and how do you consider Maintenance of software will circumvent those obstacles?
<--- Score

32. Who needs budgets?
<--- Score

33. What is the extent or complexity of the Maintenance of software problem?
<--- Score

34. Are you dealing with any of the same issues today as yesterday? What can you do about this?
<--- Score

35. What Maintenance of software events should you attend?
<--- Score

36. What Maintenance of software capabilities do you need?
<--- Score

37. Are your goals realistic? Do you need to redefine your problem? Perhaps the problem has changed or maybe you have reached your goal and need to set a new one?
<--- Score

38. Who should resolve the Maintenance of software issues?
<--- Score

39. What is the recognized need?
<--- Score

40. What are your needs in relation to Maintenance of software skills, labor, equipment, and markets?
<--- Score

41. Is the quality assurance team identified?
<--- Score

42. For your Maintenance of software project, identify and describe the business environment, is there more than one layer to the business environment?
<--- Score

43. What is the problem or issue?
<--- Score

44. What is the problem and/or vulnerability?
<--- Score

45. Which information does the Maintenance of software business case need to include?
<--- Score

46. Is it clear when you think of the day ahead of you what activities and tasks you need to complete?
<--- Score

47. Are there recognized Maintenance of software problems?
<--- Score

48. How are the Maintenance of software's objectives aligned to the group's overall stakeholder strategy?
<--- Score

49. What else needs to be measured?
<--- Score

50. Do you need to avoid or amend any Maintenance of software activities?
<--- Score

51. Consider your own Maintenance of software

project, what types of organizational problems do you think might be causing or affecting your problem, based on the work done so far?
<--- Score

52. Are controls defined to recognize and contain problems?
<--- Score

53. How can auditing be a preventative security measure?
<--- Score

54. Have you identified your Maintenance of software key performance indicators?
<--- Score

55. Who needs to know?
<--- Score

56. Whom do you really need or want to serve?
<--- Score

57. What is the Maintenance of software problem definition? What do you need to resolve?
<--- Score

58. Does your organization need more Maintenance of software education?
<--- Score

59. Where is training needed?
<--- Score

60. What should be considered when identifying available resources, constraints, and deadlines?

<--- Score

61. What is the smallest subset of the problem you can usefully solve?
<--- Score

62. What are the timeframes required to resolve each of the issues/problems?
<--- Score

63. What resources or support might you need?
<--- Score

64. Are there regulatory / compliance issues?
<--- Score

65. What do you need to start doing?
<--- Score

66. What are the stakeholder objectives to be achieved with Maintenance of software?
<--- Score

67. How do you recognize an Maintenance of software objection?
<--- Score

68. How do you take a forward-looking perspective in identifying Maintenance of software research related to market response and models?
<--- Score

69. Why is this needed?
<--- Score

70. How are training requirements identified?
<--- Score

71. What information do users need?
<--- Score

72. What tools and technologies are needed for a custom Maintenance of software project?
<--- Score

73. Who needs to know about Maintenance of software?
<--- Score

74. Does Maintenance of software create potential expectations in other areas that need to be recognized and considered?
<--- Score

75. What are the clients issues and concerns?
<--- Score

76. Which needs are not included or involved?
<--- Score

77. Do you have/need 24-hour access to key personnel?
<--- Score

78. Who needs what information?
<--- Score

79. Think about the people you identified for your Maintenance of software project and the project responsibilities you would assign to them, what kind of training do you think they would need to perform

these responsibilities effectively?
<--- Score

80. Are employees recognized for desired behaviors?
<--- Score

81. What are the Maintenance of software resources needed?
<--- Score

82. How do you identify the kinds of information that you will need?
<--- Score

83. How does it fit into your organizational needs and tasks?
<--- Score

84. Looking at each person individually – does every one have the qualities which are needed to work in this group?
<--- Score

85. What do employees need in the short term?
<--- Score

86. What are the expected benefits of Maintenance of software to the stakeholder?
<--- Score

87. Are there any specific expectations or concerns about the Maintenance of software team, Maintenance of software itself?
<--- Score

88. Is the need for organizational change recognized?
<--- Score

89. As a sponsor, customer or management, how important is it to meet goals, objectives?
<--- Score

90. Did you miss any major Maintenance of software issues?
<--- Score

91. Do you recognize Maintenance of software achievements?
<--- Score

92. How many trainings, in total, are needed?
<--- Score

93. Are there any revenue recognition issues?
<--- Score

94. Will Maintenance of software deliverables need to be tested and, if so, by whom?
<--- Score

95. Who defines the rules in relation to any given issue?
<--- Score

96. What needs to be done?
<--- Score

97. How much are sponsors, customers, partners, stakeholders involved in Maintenance of software? In other words, what are the risks, if Maintenance of software does not deliver successfully?

<--- Score

Add up total points for this section:
_____ = Total points for this section

Divided by: _____ (number of
statements answered) = _____
Average score for this section

Transfer your score to the Maintenance
of software Index at the beginning of
the Self-Assessment.

CRITERION #2: DEFINE:

INTENT: Formulate the stakeholder problem. Define the problem, needs and objectives.

In my belief, the answer to this question is clearly defined:

5 Strongly Agree

4 Agree

3 Neutral

2 Disagree

1 Strongly Disagree

1. How was the 'as is' process map developed, reviewed, verified and validated?
<--- Score

2. What defines best in class?
<--- Score

3. How will the Maintenance of software team and the group measure complete success of Maintenance of

software?
<--- Score

4. How and when will the baselines be defined?
<--- Score

5. Is there a completed SIPOC representation, describing the Suppliers, Inputs, Process, Outputs, and Customers?
<--- Score

6. What is in scope?
<--- Score

7. What is out of scope?
<--- Score

8. How is the team tracking and documenting its work?
<--- Score

9. What information do you gather?
<--- Score

10. Are all requirements met?
<--- Score

11. Has the Maintenance of software work been fairly and/or equitably divided and delegated among team members who are qualified and capable to perform the work? Has everyone contributed?
<--- Score

12. Are task requirements clearly defined?
<--- Score

13. What is the definition of Maintenance of software excellence?

<--- Score

14. What are the record-keeping requirements of Maintenance of software activities?

<--- Score

15. How will variation in the actual durations of each activity be dealt with to ensure that the expected Maintenance of software results are met?

<--- Score

16. What is the worst case scenario?

<--- Score

17. Are required metrics defined, what are they?

<--- Score

18. What are the requirements for audit information?

<--- Score

19. Are the Maintenance of software requirements testable?

<--- Score

20. How do you manage scope?

<--- Score

21. Is it clearly defined in and to your organization what you do?

<--- Score

22. What Maintenance of software services do you require?

<--- Score

23. Will team members perform Maintenance of software work when assigned and in a timely fashion?
<--- Score

24. Is special Maintenance of software user knowledge required?
<--- Score

25. Is the current 'as is' process being followed? If not, what are the discrepancies?
<--- Score

26. What intelligence can you gather?
<--- Score

27. Is there regularly 100% attendance at the team meetings? If not, have appointed substitutes attended to preserve cross-functionality and full representation?
<--- Score

28. Has everyone on the team, including the team leaders, been properly trained?
<--- Score

29. Is data collected and displayed to better understand customer(s) critical needs and requirements.
<--- Score

30. If substitutes have been appointed, have they been briefed on the Maintenance of software goals and received regular communications as to the progress to date?
<--- Score

31. Is the team formed and are team leaders (Coaches and Management Leads) assigned?
<--- Score

32. Why are you doing Maintenance of software and what is the scope?
<--- Score

33. What sort of initial information to gather?
<--- Score

34. How would you define Maintenance of software leadership?
<--- Score

35. Who is gathering Maintenance of software information?
<--- Score

36. Is the work to date meeting requirements?
<--- Score

37. Have specific policy objectives been defined?
<--- Score

38. Has your scope been defined?
<--- Score

39. What constraints exist that might impact the team?
<--- Score

40. Is the improvement team aware of the different versions of a process: what they think it is vs. what it actually is vs. what it should be vs. what it could be?

<--- Score

41. Has a team charter been developed and communicated?
<--- Score

42. What critical content must be communicated – who, what, when, where, and how?
<--- Score

43. How do you manage changes in Maintenance of software requirements?
<--- Score

44. Are there any constraints known that bear on the ability to perform Maintenance of software work? How is the team addressing them?
<--- Score

45. Are different versions of process maps needed to account for the different types of inputs?
<--- Score

46. What would be the goal or target for a Maintenance of software's improvement team?
<--- Score

47. What are the boundaries of the scope? What is in bounds and what is not? What is the start point? What is the stop point?
<--- Score

48. When is the estimated completion date?
<--- Score

49. Who are the Maintenance of software

improvement team members, including Management Leads and Coaches?

<--- Score

50. How do you catch Maintenance of software definition inconsistencies?

<--- Score

51. When are meeting minutes sent out? Who is on the distribution list?

<--- Score

52. Are accountability and ownership for Maintenance of software clearly defined?

<--- Score

53. Is there a Maintenance of software management charter, including stakeholder case, problem and goal statements, scope, milestones, roles and responsibilities, communication plan?

<--- Score

54. The political context: who holds power?

<--- Score

55. How can the value of Maintenance of software be defined?

<--- Score

56. Has/have the customer(s) been identified?

<--- Score

57. What is the scope of the Maintenance of software work?

<--- Score

58. Is the team sponsored by a champion or stakeholder leader?
<--- Score

59. Will a Maintenance of software production readiness review be required?
<--- Score

60. What are the Roles and Responsibilities for each team member and its leadership? Where is this documented?
<--- Score

61. What happens if Maintenance of software's scope changes?
<--- Score

62. Has a project plan, Gantt chart, or similar been developed/completed?
<--- Score

63. Do you have organizational privacy requirements?
<--- Score

64. Is the team equipped with available and reliable resources?
<--- Score

65. Are approval levels defined for contracts and supplements to contracts?
<--- Score

66. Where can you gather more information?
<--- Score

67. What is the context?

<--- Score

68. What gets examined?
<--- Score

69. Have all of the relationships been defined properly?
<--- Score

70. Is the team adequately staffed with the desired cross-functionality? If not, what additional resources are available to the team?
<--- Score

71. Is the Maintenance of software scope complete and appropriately sized?
<--- Score

72. How do you gather Maintenance of software requirements?
<--- Score

73. What baselines are required to be defined and managed?
<--- Score

74. Is there a clear Maintenance of software case definition?
<--- Score

75. Does the scope remain the same?
<--- Score

76. How would you define the culture at your organization, how susceptible is it to Maintenance of software changes?

<--- Score

77. How do you hand over Maintenance of software context?

<--- Score

78. What system do you use for gathering Maintenance of software information?

<--- Score

79. What are the Maintenance of software tasks and definitions?

<--- Score

80. In what way can you redefine the criteria of choice clients have in your category in your favor?

<--- Score

81. How do you keep key subject matter experts in the loop?

<--- Score

82. Is there a critical path to deliver Maintenance of software results?

<--- Score

83. Is there a completed, verified, and validated high-level 'as is' (not 'should be' or 'could be') stakeholder process map?

<--- Score

84. What sources do you use to gather information for a Maintenance of software study?

<--- Score

85. Do you have a Maintenance of software success

story or case study ready to tell and share?
<--- Score

86. Is there any additional Maintenance of software definition of success?
<--- Score

87. What specifically is the problem? Where does it occur? When does it occur? What is its extent?
<--- Score

88. What is a worst-case scenario for losses?
<--- Score

89. Has the direction changed at all during the course of Maintenance of software? If so, when did it change and why?
<--- Score

90. What is in the scope and what is not in scope?
<--- Score

91. What are the rough order estimates on cost savings/opportunities that Maintenance of software brings?
<--- Score

92. Has a high-level 'as is' process map been completed, verified and validated?
<--- Score

93. Is the scope of Maintenance of software defined?
<--- Score

94. Is Maintenance of software required?
<--- Score

95. Does the team have regular meetings?
<--- Score

96. What are the dynamics of the communication plan?
<--- Score

97. Has a Maintenance of software requirement not been met?
<--- Score

98. How are consistent Maintenance of software definitions important?
<--- Score

99. Are roles and responsibilities formally defined?
<--- Score

100. Is the Maintenance of software scope manageable?
<--- Score

101. What are (control) requirements for Maintenance of software Information?
<--- Score

102. What is the definition of success?
<--- Score

103. What Maintenance of software requirements should be gathered?
<--- Score

104. What customer feedback methods were used to solicit their input?

<--- Score

105. What key stakeholder process output measure(s) does Maintenance of software leverage and how?
<--- Score

106. Are there different segments of customers?
<--- Score

107. Is Maintenance of software linked to key stakeholder goals and objectives?
<--- Score

108. Are customer(s) identified and segmented according to their different needs and requirements?
<--- Score

109. What is the scope of Maintenance of software?
<--- Score

110. How do you manage unclear Maintenance of software requirements?
<--- Score

111. Are audit criteria, scope, frequency and methods defined?
<--- Score

112. What is out-of-scope initially?
<--- Score

113. Scope of sensitive information?
<--- Score

114. Will team members regularly document their Maintenance of software work?

<--- Score

115. What are the Maintenance of software use cases?
<--- Score

116. When is/was the Maintenance of software start date?
<--- Score

117. Is full participation by members in regularly held team meetings guaranteed?
<--- Score

118. Has anyone else (internal or external to the group) attempted to solve this problem or a similar one before? If so, what knowledge can be leveraged from these previous efforts?
<--- Score

119. How did the Maintenance of software manager receive input to the development of a Maintenance of software improvement plan and the estimated completion dates/times of each activity?
<--- Score

120. What are the core elements of the Maintenance of software business case?
<--- Score

121. Have all basic functions of Maintenance of software been defined?
<--- Score

122. How do you gather requirements?
<--- Score

123. Has the improvement team collected the 'voice of the customer' (obtained feedback – qualitative and quantitative)?
<--- Score

124. Have the customer needs been translated into specific, measurable requirements? How?
<--- Score

125. Are resources adequate for the scope?
<--- Score

126. What is the scope of the Maintenance of software effort?
<--- Score

127. Do you all define Maintenance of software in the same way?
<--- Score

128. Are improvement team members fully trained on Maintenance of software?
<--- Score

129. How often are the team meetings?
<--- Score

130. Are the Maintenance of software requirements complete?
<--- Score

131. How does the Maintenance of software manager ensure against scope creep?
<--- Score

132. Is Maintenance of software currently on schedule

according to the plan?
<--- Score

133. What are the tasks and definitions?
<--- Score

134. What are the compelling stakeholder reasons for embarking on Maintenance of software?
<--- Score

135. Do the problem and goal statements meet the SMART criteria (specific, measurable, attainable, relevant, and time-bound)?
<--- Score

136. What was the context?
<--- Score

137. Who is gathering information?
<--- Score

138. What scope to assess?
<--- Score

139. Is scope creep really all bad news?
<--- Score

140. Who defines (or who defined) the rules and roles?
<--- Score

Add up total points for this section:
_ _ _ _ _ = Total points for this section

Divided by: _ _ _ _ _ _ (number of statements answered) = _ _ _ _ _ _
Average score for this section

Transfer your score to the Maintenance
of software Index at the beginning of
the Self-Assessment.

CRITERION #3: MEASURE:

INTENT: Gather the correct data. Measure the current performance and evolution of the situation.

In my belief, the answer to this question is clearly defined:

5 Strongly Agree

4 Agree

3 Neutral

2 Disagree

1 Strongly Disagree

1. How do you verify the Maintenance of software requirements quality?
<--- Score

2. How will success or failure be measured?
<--- Score

3. How do you measure success?
<--- Score

4. Do you have an issue in getting priority?
<--- Score

5. Who should receive measurement reports?
<--- Score

6. How do you verify if Maintenance of software is built right?
<--- Score

7. What are the strategic priorities for this year?
<--- Score

8. What drives O&M cost?
<--- Score

9. What happens if cost savings do not materialize?
<--- Score

10. Are the units of measure consistent?
<--- Score

11. How will you measure your Maintenance of software effectiveness?
<--- Score

12. How can you measure the performance?
<--- Score

13. What are the estimated costs of proposed changes?
<--- Score

14. Which Maintenance of software impacts are significant?

<--- Score

15. Are the Maintenance of software benefits worth its costs?
<--- Score

16. Are you able to realize any cost savings?
<--- Score

17. How can you reduce costs?
<--- Score

18. What are the costs of delaying Maintenance of software action?
<--- Score

19. When should you bother with diagrams?
<--- Score

20. Will Maintenance of software have an impact on current business continuity, disaster recovery processes and/or infrastructure?
<--- Score

21. How will costs be allocated?
<--- Score

22. Do you have a flow diagram of what happens?
<--- Score

23. What potential environmental factors impact the Maintenance of software effort?
<--- Score

24. What is measured? Why?
<--- Score

25. What details are required of the Maintenance of software cost structure?
<--- Score

26. Are you aware of what could cause a problem?
<--- Score

27. Who pays the cost?
<--- Score

28. What does your operating model cost?
<--- Score

29. What harm might be caused?
<--- Score

30. How do you verify and develop ideas and innovations?
<--- Score

31. At what cost?
<--- Score

32. What tests verify requirements?
<--- Score

33. What are allowable costs?
<--- Score

34. How do you quantify and qualify impacts?
<--- Score

35. What are your operating costs?
<--- Score

36. What causes mismanagement?

<--- Score

37. How are costs allocated?

<--- Score

38. How do you aggregate measures across priorities?

<--- Score

39. How do you verify and validate the Maintenance of software data?

<--- Score

40. What is an unallowable cost?

<--- Score

41. What could cause delays in the schedule?

<--- Score

42. How will effects be measured?

<--- Score

43. How sensitive must the Maintenance of software strategy be to cost?

<--- Score

44. How do you prevent mis-estimating cost?

<--- Score

45. Does management have the right priorities among projects?

<--- Score

46. How will measures be used to manage and adapt?

<--- Score

47. What users will be impacted?

<--- Score

48. How will you measure success?

<--- Score

49. Are Maintenance of software vulnerabilities categorized and prioritized?

<--- Score

50. Are there competing Maintenance of software priorities?

<--- Score

51. Are supply costs steady or fluctuating?

<--- Score

52. Why do the measurements/indicators matter?

<--- Score

53. What can be used to verify compliance?

<--- Score

54. What do you measure and why?

<--- Score

55. What is the total cost related to deploying Maintenance of software, including any consulting or professional services?

<--- Score

56. How will your organization measure success?

<--- Score

57. Where is the cost?

<--- Score

58. Does a Maintenance of software quantification method exist?
<--- Score

59. What does losing customers cost your organization?
<--- Score

60. How do you measure efficient delivery of Maintenance of software services?
<--- Score

61. What would be a real cause for concern?
<--- Score

62. How do your measurements capture actionable Maintenance of software information for use in exceeding your customers expectations and securing your customers engagement?
<--- Score

63. What causes innovation to fail or succeed in your organization?
<--- Score

64. Does the Maintenance of software task fit the client's priorities?
<--- Score

65. Are you taking your company in the direction of better and revenue or cheaper and cost?
<--- Score

66. What measurements are possible, practicable and

meaningful?

<--- Score

67. Do the benefits outweigh the costs?

<--- Score

68. What are the costs?

<--- Score

69. Have you included everything in your Maintenance of software cost models?

<--- Score

70. Which costs should be taken into account?

<--- Score

71. How do you measure variability?

<--- Score

72. What is your decision requirements diagram?

<--- Score

73. How can you reduce the costs of obtaining inputs?

<--- Score

74. What is the root cause(s) of the problem?

<--- Score

75. Are missed Maintenance of software opportunities costing your organization money?

<--- Score

76. What relevant entities could be measured?

<--- Score

77. How do you verify your resources?

<--- Score

78. What are the current costs of the Maintenance of software process?
<--- Score

79. What would it cost to replace your technology?
<--- Score

80. Among the Maintenance of software product and service cost to be estimated, which is considered hardest to estimate?
<--- Score

81. How to cause the change?
<--- Score

82. Do you aggressively reward and promote the people who have the biggest impact on creating excellent Maintenance of software services/ products?
<--- Score

83. What do people want to verify?
<--- Score

84. Do you effectively measure and reward individual and team performance?
<--- Score

85. Why do you expend time and effort to implement measurement, for whom?
<--- Score

86. What methods are feasible and acceptable to estimate the impact of reforms?

<--- Score

87. What measurements are being captured?
<--- Score

88. What are your primary costs, revenues, assets?
<--- Score

89. Do you have any cost Maintenance of software limitation requirements?
<--- Score

90. How is performance measured?
<--- Score

91. Have you made assumptions about the shape of the future, particularly its impact on your customers and competitors?
<--- Score

92. What does a Test Case verify?
<--- Score

93. What causes extra work or rework?
<--- Score

94. How do you verify the authenticity of the data and information used?
<--- Score

95. What are the Maintenance of software investment costs?
<--- Score

96. Have design-to-cost goals been established?
<--- Score

97. Is the solution cost-effective?

<--- Score

98. What are the costs and benefits?

<--- Score

99. Is the cost worth the Maintenance of software effort ?

<--- Score

100. What evidence is there and what is measured?

<--- Score

101. How do you verify performance?

<--- Score

102. Are the measurements objective?

<--- Score

103. How are measurements made?

<--- Score

104. How is progress measured?

<--- Score

105. What are your customers expectations and measures?

<--- Score

106. What are the types and number of measures to use?

<--- Score

107. How much does it cost?

<--- Score

108. How do you measure lifecycle phases?
<--- Score

109. What are the Maintenance of software key cost drivers?
<--- Score

110. How do you control the overall costs of your work processes?
<--- Score

111. How can you manage cost down?
<--- Score

112. How can a Maintenance of software test verify your ideas or assumptions?
<--- Score

113. What are the costs of reform?
<--- Score

114. What is the Maintenance of software business impact?
<--- Score

115. When are costs are incurred?
<--- Score

116. What is your Maintenance of software quality cost segregation study?
<--- Score

117. Are actual costs in line with budgeted costs?
<--- Score

118. Are there any easy-to-implement alternatives to Maintenance of software? Sometimes other solutions are available that do not require the cost implications of a full-blown project?
<--- Score

119. Was a business case (cost/benefit) developed?
<--- Score

120. Is there an opportunity to verify requirements?
<--- Score

121. Are there measurements based on task performance?
<--- Score

122. What are hidden Maintenance of software quality costs?
<--- Score

123. What disadvantage does this cause for the user?
<--- Score

124. What causes investor action?
<--- Score

125. Has a cost center been established?
<--- Score

126. What could cause you to change course?
<--- Score

127. What are the operational costs after Maintenance of software deployment?

<--- Score

128. What are the uncertainties surrounding estimates of impact?
<--- Score

129. Did you tackle the cause or the symptom?
<--- Score

130. What are your key Maintenance of software organizational performance measures, including key short and longer-term financial measures?
<--- Score

Add up total points for this section:
_ _ _ _ _ = Total points for this section

Divided by: _ _ _ _ _ _ (number of statements answered) = _ _ _ _ _ _
Average score for this section

Transfer your score to the Maintenance of software Index at the beginning of the Self-Assessment.

CRITERION #4: ANALYZE:

INTENT: Analyze causes, assumptions
and hypotheses.

In my belief, the answer to this
question is clearly defined:

5 Strongly Agree

4 Agree

3 Neutral

2 Disagree

1 Strongly Disagree

1. What are your best practices for minimizing
Maintenance of software project risk, while
demonstrating incremental value and quick wins
throughout the Maintenance of software project
lifecycle?
<--- Score

2. Do you understand your management processes
today?
<--- Score

3. What other jobs or tasks affect the performance of the steps in the Maintenance of software process?

<--- Score

4. Do you, as a leader, bounce back quickly from setbacks?

<--- Score

5. Are all staff in core Maintenance of software subjects Highly Qualified?

<--- Score

6. How was the detailed process map generated, verified, and validated?

<--- Score

7. How much data can be collected in the given timeframe?

<--- Score

8. How do you use Maintenance of software data and information to support organizational decision making and innovation?

<--- Score

9. What is the Value Stream Mapping?

<--- Score

10. How is Maintenance of software data gathered?

<--- Score

11. What qualifies as competition?

<--- Score

12. What Maintenance of software metrics are outputs of the process?

<--- Score

13. How is the way you as the leader think and process information affecting your organizational culture?

<--- Score

14. What are your current levels and trends in key Maintenance of software measures or indicators of product and process performance that are important to and directly serve your customers?

<--- Score

15. What qualifications do Maintenance of software leaders need?

<--- Score

16. What resources go in to get the desired output?

<--- Score

17. An organizationally feasible system request is one that considers the mission, goals and objectives of the organization, key questions are: is the Maintenance of software solution request practical and will it solve a problem or take advantage of an opportunity to achieve company goals?

<--- Score

18. When should a process be art not science?

<--- Score

19. Was a cause-and-effect diagram used to explore the different types of causes (or sources of variation)?

<--- Score

20. Were Pareto charts (or similar) used to portray the 'heavy hitters' (or key sources of variation)?
<--- Score

21. How do you measure the operational performance of your key work systems and processes, including productivity, cycle time, and other appropriate measures of process effectiveness, efficiency, and innovation?
<--- Score

22. Has an output goal been set?
<--- Score

23. Do your leaders quickly bounce back from setbacks?
<--- Score

24. What successful thing are you doing today that may be blinding you to new growth opportunities?
<--- Score

25. How will the data be checked for quality?
<--- Score

26. What Maintenance of software data should be managed?
<--- Score

27. Is data and process analysis, root cause analysis and quantifying the gap/opportunity in place?
<--- Score

28. What is the cost of poor quality as supported by the team's analysis?

<--- Score

29. How does the organization define, manage, and improve its Maintenance of software processes?
<--- Score

30. Is there any way to speed up the process?
<--- Score

31. Is there an established change management process?
<--- Score

32. Are gaps between current performance and the goal performance identified?
<--- Score

33. Record-keeping requirements flow from the records needed as inputs, outputs, controls and for transformation of a Maintenance of software process, are the records needed as inputs to the Maintenance of software process available?
<--- Score

34. What were the crucial 'moments of truth' on the process map?
<--- Score

35. What are the disruptive Maintenance of software technologies that enable your organization to radically change your business processes?
<--- Score

36. What types of data do your Maintenance of software indicators require?
<--- Score

37. Was a detailed process map created to amplify critical steps of the 'as is' stakeholder process?
<--- Score

38. How many input/output points does it require?
<--- Score

39. How has the Maintenance of software data been gathered?
<--- Score

40. What output to create?
<--- Score

41. What tools were used to narrow the list of possible causes?
<--- Score

42. What qualifications are needed?
<--- Score

43. What other organizational variables, such as reward systems or communication systems, affect the performance of this Maintenance of software process?
<--- Score

44. Have the problem and goal statements been updated to reflect the additional knowledge gained from the analyze phase?
<--- Score

45. What data do you need to collect?
<--- Score

46. What are the best opportunities for value

improvement?
<--- Score

47. What Maintenance of software data do you gather or use now?
<--- Score

48. Is the final output clearly identified?
<--- Score

49. What information qualified as important?
<--- Score

50. How do you define collaboration and team output?
<--- Score

51. Think about the functions involved in your Maintenance of software project, what processes flow from these functions?
<--- Score

52. What is the oversight process?
<--- Score

53. How do you promote understanding that opportunity for improvement is not criticism of the status quo, or the people who created the status quo?
<--- Score

54. Is there a strict change management process?
<--- Score

55. Is the performance gap determined?
<--- Score

56. How do mission and objectives affect the Maintenance of software processes of your organization?

<--- Score

57. What qualifications are necessary?

<--- Score

58. Were there any improvement opportunities identified from the process analysis?

<--- Score

59. What does the data say about the performance of the stakeholder process?

<--- Score

60. Do quality systems drive continuous improvement?

<--- Score

61. How do you implement and manage your work processes to ensure that they meet design requirements?

<--- Score

62. What Maintenance of software data should be collected?

<--- Score

63. What did the team gain from developing a sub-process map?

<--- Score

64. What are your outputs?

<--- Score

65. What process improvements will be needed?
<--- Score

66. What is your organizations system for selecting qualified vendors?
<--- Score

67. Have any additional benefits been identified that will result from closing all or most of the gaps?
<--- Score

68. Are all team members qualified for all tasks?
<--- Score

69. What kind of crime could a potential new hire have committed that would not only not disqualify him/her from being hired by your organization, but would actually indicate that he/she might be a particularly good fit?
<--- Score

70. What systems/processes must you excel at?
<--- Score

71. Has data output been validated?
<--- Score

72. Which Maintenance of software data should be retained?
<--- Score

73. What are evaluation criteria for the output?
<--- Score

74. What are the revised rough estimates of the financial savings/opportunity for Maintenance of

software improvements?
<--- Score

75. How do your work systems and key work processes relate to and capitalize on your core competencies?
<--- Score

76. How do you identify specific Maintenance of software investment opportunities and emerging trends?
<--- Score

77. Who qualifies to gain access to data?
<--- Score

78. What do you need to qualify?
<--- Score

79. How do you ensure that the Maintenance of software opportunity is realistic?
<--- Score

80. Did any value-added analysis or 'lean thinking' take place to identify some of the gaps shown on the 'as is' process map?
<--- Score

81. What are your Maintenance of software processes?
<--- Score

82. Do your employees have the opportunity to do what they do best everyday?
<--- Score

83. What are the Maintenance of software business

drivers?
<--- Score

84. How is data used for program management and improvement?
<--- Score

85. How is the Maintenance of software Value Stream Mapping managed?
<--- Score

86. Identify an operational issue in your organization, for example, could a particular task be done more quickly or more efficiently by Maintenance of software?
<--- Score

87. Who will gather what data?
<--- Score

88. What internal processes need improvement?
<--- Score

89. What conclusions were drawn from the team's data collection and analysis? How did the team reach these conclusions?
<--- Score

90. What qualifications and skills do you need?
<--- Score

91. How often will data be collected for measures?
<--- Score

92. Can you add value to the current Maintenance of software decision-making process (largely qualitative)

by incorporating uncertainty modeling (more quantitative)?
<--- Score

93. Should you invest in industry-recognized qualifications?
<--- Score

94. Have you defined which data is gathered how?
<--- Score

95. Who gets your output?
<--- Score

96. Where can you get qualified talent today?
<--- Score

97. Is the gap/opportunity displayed and communicated in financial terms?
<--- Score

98. Who is involved with workflow mapping?
<--- Score

99. What will drive Maintenance of software change?
<--- Score

100. What process should you select for improvement?
<--- Score

101. What are the processes for audit reporting and management?
<--- Score

102. How is the data gathered?

<--- Score

103. What are your current levels and trends in key measures or indicators of Maintenance of software product and process performance that are important to and directly serve your customers? How do these results compare with the performance of your competitors and other organizations with similar offerings?
<--- Score

104. What tools were used to generate the list of possible causes?
<--- Score

105. Who owns what data?
<--- Score

106. What, related to, Maintenance of software processes does your organization outsource?
<--- Score

107. Where is the data coming from to measure compliance?
<--- Score

108. What controls do you have in place to protect data?
<--- Score

109. What were the financial benefits resulting from any 'ground fruit or low-hanging fruit' (quick fixes)?
<--- Score

110. Are you missing Maintenance of software opportunities?

<--- Score

111. Where is Maintenance of software data gathered?
<--- Score

112. Do your contracts/agreements contain data security obligations?
<--- Score

113. Do several people in different organizational units assist with the Maintenance of software process?
<--- Score

114. How will corresponding data be collected?
<--- Score

115. What are the personnel training and qualifications required?
<--- Score

116. Is the required Maintenance of software data gathered?
<--- Score

117. What quality tools were used to get through the analyze phase?
<--- Score

118. What is the Maintenance of software Driver?
<--- Score

119. Were any designed experiments used to generate additional insight into the data analysis?
<--- Score

120. Did any additional data need to be collected?

<--- Score

121. How will the change process be managed?
<--- Score

122. What Maintenance of software data will be collected?
<--- Score

123. How can risk management be tied procedurally to process elements?
<--- Score

124. What data is gathered?
<--- Score

125. Are your outputs consistent?
<--- Score

126. What is the complexity of the output produced?
<--- Score

127. What are the necessary qualifications?
<--- Score

128. Are Maintenance of software changes recognized early enough to be approved through the regular process?
<--- Score

129. Think about some of the processes you undertake within your organization, which do you own?
<--- Score

130. Do you have the authority to produce the

output?

<--- Score

131. A compounding model resolution with available relevant data can often provide insight towards a solution methodology; which Maintenance of software models, tools and techniques are necessary?

<--- Score

132. Is the Maintenance of software process severely broken such that a re-design is necessary?

<--- Score

133. What training and qualifications will you need?

<--- Score

134. What are your key performance measures or indicators and in-process measures for the control and improvement of your Maintenance of software processes?

<--- Score

135. Is the suppliers process defined and controlled?

<--- Score

136. How will the Maintenance of software data be captured?

<--- Score

Add up total points for this section:
_ _ _ _ _ = Total points for this section

Divided by: _ _ _ _ _ _ (number of

statements answered) = _ _ _ _ _ _
Average score for this section

Transfer your score to the Maintenance
of software Index at the beginning of
the Self-Assessment.

CRITERION #5: IMPROVE:

INTENT: Develop a practical solution. Innovate, establish and test the solution and to measure the results.

In my belief, the answer to this question is clearly defined:

5 Strongly Agree

4 Agree

3 Neutral

2 Disagree

1 Strongly Disagree

1. How significant is the improvement in the eyes of the end user?
<--- Score

2. Who are the Maintenance of software decision makers?
<--- Score

3. What tools do you use once you have decided

on a Maintenance of software strategy and more importantly how do you choose?
<--- Score

4. What are the affordable Maintenance of software risks?

<--- Score

5. Maintenance of software risk decisions: whose call Is It?
<--- Score

6. How do the Maintenance of software results compare with the performance of your competitors and other organizations with similar offerings?
<--- Score

7. What needs improvement? Why?

<--- Score

8. What are the concrete Maintenance of software results?
<--- Score

9. What are the implications of the one critical Maintenance of software decision 10 minutes, 10 months, and 10 years from now?
<--- Score

10. What were the criteria for evaluating a Maintenance of software pilot?

<--- Score

11. When you map the key players in your own work and the types/domains of relationships with them, which relationships do you find easy and

which challenging, and why?
<--- Score

12. Are risk management tasks balanced centrally and locally?
<--- Score

13. What tools were used to tap into the creativity and encourage 'outside the box' thinking?
<--- Score

14. Are procedures documented for managing Maintenance of software risks?
<--- Score

15. What is the team's contingency plan for potential problems occurring in implementation?
<--- Score

16. Who makes the Maintenance of software decisions in your organization?
<--- Score

17. How do you manage Maintenance of software risk?
<--- Score

18. What area needs the greatest improvement?
<--- Score

19. Are decisions made in a timely manner?
<--- Score

20. How will you recognize and celebrate results?
<--- Score

21. What alternative responses are available to manage risk?
<--- Score

22. Can the solution be designed and implemented within an acceptable time period?
<--- Score

23. What were the underlying assumptions on the cost-benefit analysis?
<--- Score

24. What tools were most useful during the improve phase?
<--- Score

25. How can you improve Maintenance of software?
<--- Score

26. How do you decide how much to remunerate an employee?
<--- Score

27. Risk events: what are the things that could go wrong?
<--- Score

28. Have you identified breakpoints and/or risk tolerances that will trigger broad consideration of a potential need for intervention or modification of strategy?
<--- Score

29. How can you improve performance?
<--- Score

30. Who will be responsible for making the decisions to include or exclude requested changes once Maintenance of software is underway?
<--- Score

31. Do you have the optimal project management team structure?
<--- Score

32. Is supporting Maintenance of software documentation required?
<--- Score

33. For estimation problems, how do you develop an estimation statement?
<--- Score

34. Does a good decision guarantee a good outcome?
<--- Score

35. Who are the key stakeholders for the Maintenance of software evaluation?
<--- Score

36. Who will be responsible for documenting the Maintenance of software requirements in detail?
<--- Score

37. Is the solution technically practical?
<--- Score

38. How will you know that a change is an improvement?
<--- Score

39. How do you define the solutions' scope?
<--- Score

40. What went well, what should change, what can improve?
<--- Score

41. What lessons, if any, from a pilot were incorporated into the design of the full-scale solution?
<--- Score

42. Are risk triggers captured?
<--- Score

43. How do you measure progress and evaluate training effectiveness?
<--- Score

44. How does your organization evaluate strategic Maintenance of software success?
<--- Score

45. Who will be using the results of the measurement activities?
<--- Score

46. What is Maintenance of software's impact on utilizing the best solution(s)?
<--- Score

47. Why improve in the first place?
<--- Score

48. How are Maintenance of software risks managed?
<--- Score

49. How do you measure improved Maintenance of software service perception, and satisfaction?
<--- Score

50. Do you cover the five essential competencies: Communication, Collaboration,Innovation, Adaptability, and Leadership that improve an organizations ability to leverage the new Maintenance of software in a volatile global economy?
<--- Score

51. How will you know when its improved?
<--- Score

52. Are the most efficient solutions problem-specific?
<--- Score

53. Is there any other Maintenance of software solution?
<--- Score

54. What Maintenance of software improvements can be made?
<--- Score

55. Which of the recognised risks out of all risks can be most likely transferred?
<--- Score

56. Who do you report Maintenance of software results to?
<--- Score

57. Are events managed to resolution?
<--- Score

58. Do those selected for the Maintenance of software team have a good general understanding of what Maintenance of software is all about?
<--- Score

59. What practices helps your organization to develop its capacity to recognize patterns?
<--- Score

60. Risk Identification: What are the possible risk events your organization faces in relation to Maintenance of software?
<--- Score

61. What current systems have to be understood and/or changed?
<--- Score

62. Who should make the Maintenance of software decisions?
<--- Score

63. How will you know that you have improved?
<--- Score

64. How do you improve Maintenance of software service perception, and satisfaction?
<--- Score

65. Are you assessing Maintenance of software and risk?
<--- Score

66. What are your current levels and trends in key measures or indicators of workforce and leader development?

<--- Score

67. Is the scope clearly documented?
<--- Score

68. Who are the people involved in developing and implementing Maintenance of software?
<--- Score

69. What can you do to improve?
<--- Score

70. Are the risks fully understood, reasonable and manageable?
<--- Score

71. Who controls key decisions that will be made?
<--- Score

72. How do you measure risk?
<--- Score

73. What to do with the results or outcomes of measurements?
<--- Score

74. Is any Maintenance of software documentation required?
<--- Score

75. How will you measure the results?
<--- Score

76. Risk factors: what are the characteristics of Maintenance of software that make it risky?
<--- Score

77. If you could go back in time five years, what decision would you make differently? What is your best guess as to what decision you're making today you might regret five years from now?
<--- Score

78. What is Maintenance of software risk?
<--- Score

79. To what extent does management recognize Maintenance of software as a tool to increase the results?
<--- Score

80. Does the goal represent a desired result that can be measured?
<--- Score

81. Is there a high likelihood that any recommendations will achieve their intended results?
<--- Score

82. Where do the Maintenance of software decisions reside?
<--- Score

83. How do you go about comparing Maintenance of software approaches/solutions?
<--- Score

84. What are the expected Maintenance of software results?
<--- Score

85. Who manages Maintenance of software risk?

<--- Score

86. What risks do you need to manage?
<--- Score

87. Do you combine technical expertise with business knowledge and Maintenance of software Key topics include lifecycles, development approaches, requirements and how to make a business case?
<--- Score

88. What actually has to improve and by how much?
<--- Score

89. How do you keep improving Maintenance of software?
<--- Score

90. What is the magnitude of the improvements?
<--- Score

91. What should a proof of concept or pilot accomplish?
<--- Score

92. Who manages supplier risk management in your organization?
<--- Score

93. What is the Maintenance of software's sustainability risk?
<--- Score

94. Have you achieved Maintenance of software

improvements?
<--- Score

95. What tools were used to evaluate the potential solutions?
<--- Score

96. Can you identify any significant risks or exposures to Maintenance of software third- parties (vendors, service providers, alliance partners etc) that concern you?
<--- Score

97. Is the Maintenance of software solution sustainable?
<--- Score

98. Is the measure of success for Maintenance of software understandable to a variety of people?
<--- Score

99. Where do you need Maintenance of software improvement?
<--- Score

100. Will the controls trigger any other risks?
<--- Score

101. Would you develop a Maintenance of software Communication Strategy?
<--- Score

102. For decision problems, how do you develop a decision statement?
<--- Score

103. How do you link measurement and risk?
<--- Score

104. How risky is your organization?
<--- Score

105. Is the Maintenance of software documentation thorough?
<--- Score

106. Do you need to do a usability evaluation?
<--- Score

107. How scalable is your Maintenance of software solution?
<--- Score

108. How can the phases of Maintenance of software development be identified?
<--- Score

109. How does the team improve its work?
<--- Score

110. How do you deal with Maintenance of software risk?
<--- Score

111. What do you want to improve?
<--- Score

112. Which Maintenance of software solution is appropriate?
<--- Score

113. What is the risk?

<--- Score

114. How can skill-level changes improve Maintenance of software?
<--- Score

115. Is Maintenance of software documentation maintained?
<--- Score

116. What are the Maintenance of software security risks?
<--- Score

117. Do vendor agreements bring new compliance risk ?
<--- Score

118. How risky is your organization?
<--- Score

119. How is continuous improvement applied to risk management?
<--- Score

120. How can you better manage risk?
<--- Score

121. How is knowledge sharing about risk management improved?
<--- Score

122. In the past few months, what is the smallest change you have made that has had the biggest positive result? What was it about that small change that produced the large return?

<--- Score

123. What criteria will you use to assess your Maintenance of software risks?

<--- Score

124. How do you mitigate Maintenance of software risk?

<--- Score

125. Explorations of the frontiers of Maintenance of software will help you build influence, improve Maintenance of software, optimize decision making, and sustain change, what is your approach?

<--- Score

126. What strategies for Maintenance of software improvement are successful?

<--- Score

127. How do you manage and improve your Maintenance of software work systems to deliver customer value and achieve organizational success and sustainability?

<--- Score

128. How do you improve your likelihood of success ?

<--- Score

129. Is the Maintenance of software risk managed?

<--- Score

Add up total points for this section:
_ _ _ _ _ = Total points for this section

Divided by: _____ (number of
statements answered) = _____
Average score for this section

Transfer your score to the Maintenance
of software Index at the beginning of
the Self-Assessment.

CRITERION #6: CONTROL:

INTENT: Implement the practical solution. Maintain the performance and correct possible complications.

In my belief, the answer to this question is clearly defined:

5 Strongly Agree

4 Agree

3 Neutral

2 Disagree

1 Strongly Disagree

1. Act/Adjust: What Do you Need to Do Differently?
<--- Score

2. How do you monitor usage and cost?
<--- Score

3. Are documented procedures clear and easy to follow for the operators?
<--- Score

4. How do you spread information?
<--- Score

5. What is your plan to assess your security risks?
<--- Score

6. Does the response plan contain a definite closed loop continual improvement scheme (e.g., plan-do-check-act)?
<--- Score

7. Are the planned controls in place?
<--- Score

8. Is there a recommended audit plan for routine surveillance inspections of Maintenance of software's gains?
<--- Score

9. What is the control/monitoring plan?
<--- Score

10. How will the process owner and team be able to hold the gains?
<--- Score

11. Are pertinent alerts monitored, analyzed and distributed to appropriate personnel?
<--- Score

12. Is new knowledge gained imbedded in the response plan?
<--- Score

13. How will the day-to-day responsibilities for

monitoring and continual improvement be transferred from the improvement team to the process owner?
<--- Score

14. Have new or revised work instructions resulted?
<--- Score

15. Does the Maintenance of software performance meet the customer's requirements?
<--- Score

16. What are the critical parameters to watch?
<--- Score

17. Are suggested corrective/restorative actions indicated on the response plan for known causes to problems that might surface?
<--- Score

18. How do you plan for the cost of succession?
<--- Score

19. Where do ideas that reach policy makers and planners as proposals for Maintenance of software strengthening and reform actually originate?
<--- Score

20. What other systems, operations, processes, and infrastructures (hiring practices, staffing, training, incentives/rewards, metrics/dashboards/scorecards, etc.) need updates, additions, changes, or deletions in order to facilitate knowledge transfer and improvements?
<--- Score

21. How do senior leaders actions reflect a commitment to the organizations Maintenance of software values?

<--- Score

22. How likely is the current Maintenance of software plan to come in on schedule or on budget?

<--- Score

23. Does a troubleshooting guide exist or is it needed?

<--- Score

24. What other areas of the group might benefit from the Maintenance of software team's improvements, knowledge, and learning?

<--- Score

25. How can you best use all of your knowledge repositories to enhance learning and sharing?

<--- Score

26. Are there documented procedures?

<--- Score

27. How do you encourage people to take control and responsibility?

<--- Score

28. Who is the Maintenance of software process owner?

<--- Score

29. How do you select, collect, align, and integrate Maintenance of software data and information for tracking daily operations and overall organizational performance, including progress

relative to strategic objectives and action plans?
<--- Score

30. How is Maintenance of software project cost planned, managed, monitored?
<--- Score

31. In the case of a Maintenance of software project, the criteria for the audit derive from implementation objectives, an audit of a Maintenance of software project involves assessing whether the recommendations outlined for implementation have been met, can you track that any Maintenance of software project is implemented as planned, and is it working?
<--- Score

32. How do you plan on providing proper recognition and disclosure of supporting companies?
<--- Score

33. Will existing staff require re-training, for example, to learn new business processes?
<--- Score

34. Does Maintenance of software appropriately measure and monitor risk?
<--- Score

35. Are new process steps, standards, and documentation ingrained into normal operations?
<--- Score

36. Are controls in place and consistently applied?
<--- Score

37. What key inputs and outputs are being measured on an ongoing basis?
<--- Score

38. Is there documentation that will support the successful operation of the improvement?
<--- Score

39. What quality tools were useful in the control phase?
<--- Score

40. Is a response plan established and deployed?
<--- Score

41. What are you attempting to measure/monitor?
<--- Score

42. How will the process owner verify improvement in present and future sigma levels, process capabilities?
<--- Score

43. How will Maintenance of software decisions be made and monitored?
<--- Score

44. Is there an action plan in case of emergencies?
<--- Score

45. Is there a Maintenance of software Communication plan covering who needs to get what information when?
<--- Score

46. What is your theory of human motivation, and

how does your compensation plan fit with that view?
<--- Score

47. Is there a control plan in place for sustaining improvements (short and long-term)?
<--- Score

48. What is the best design framework for Maintenance of software organization now that, in a post industrial-age if the top-down, command and control model is no longer relevant?
<--- Score

49. What do you measure to verify effectiveness gains?
<--- Score

50. What are the known security controls?
<--- Score

51. How will you measure your QA plan's effectiveness?
<--- Score

52. What should the next improvement project be that is related to Maintenance of software?
<--- Score

53. What do your reports reflect?
<--- Score

54. You may have created your quality measures at a time when you lacked resources, technology wasn't up to the required standard, or low service levels were the industry norm. Have those circumstances changed?

<--- Score

55. Who will be in control?
<--- Score

56. Implementation Planning: is a pilot needed to test the changes before a full roll out occurs?
<--- Score

57. Is there a documented and implemented monitoring plan?
<--- Score

58. Will your goals reflect your program budget?
<--- Score

59. Will any special training be provided for results interpretation?
<--- Score

60. Has the Maintenance of software value of standards been quantified?
<--- Score

61. How is change control managed?
<--- Score

62. Can support from partners be adjusted?
<--- Score

63. Do you monitor the effectiveness of your Maintenance of software activities?
<--- Score

64. Is the Maintenance of software test/monitoring cost justified?

<--- Score

65. Who has control over resources?
<--- Score

66. Who controls critical resources?
<--- Score

67. Against what alternative is success being measured?
<--- Score

68. Do the Maintenance of software decisions you make today help people and the planet tomorrow?
<--- Score

69. Is knowledge gained on process shared and institutionalized?
<--- Score

70. Are the Maintenance of software standards challenging?
<--- Score

71. What can you control?
<--- Score

72. Can you adapt and adjust to changing Maintenance of software situations?
<--- Score

73. Are the planned controls working?
<--- Score

74. Will the team be available to assist members in planning investigations?

<--- Score

75. How do your controls stack up?
<--- Score

76. What are the key elements of your Maintenance of software performance improvement system, including your evaluation, organizational learning, and innovation processes?
<--- Score

77. How do you establish and deploy modified action plans if circumstances require a shift in plans and rapid execution of new plans?
<--- Score

78. How widespread is its use?
<--- Score

79. How might the group capture best practices and lessons learned so as to leverage improvements?
<--- Score

80. Are operating procedures consistent?
<--- Score

81. Is there a standardized process?
<--- Score

82. How will input, process, and output variables be checked to detect for sub-optimal conditions?
<--- Score

83. What are customers monitoring?
<--- Score

84. Who is going to spread your message?
<--- Score

85. Has the improved process and its steps been standardized?
<--- Score

86. What adjustments to the strategies are needed?
<--- Score

87. Is there a transfer of ownership and knowledge to process owner and process team tasked with the responsibilities.
<--- Score

88. Are you measuring, monitoring and predicting Maintenance of software activities to optimize operations and profitability, and enhancing outcomes?
<--- Score

89. What is the standard for acceptable Maintenance of software performance?
<--- Score

90. What is the recommended frequency of auditing?
<--- Score

91. Do the viable solutions scale to future needs?
<--- Score

92. Is a response plan in place for when the input, process, or output measures indicate an 'out-of-control' condition?
<--- Score

93. What should you measure to verify efficiency gains?
<--- Score

94. What are the performance and scale of the Maintenance of software tools?
<--- Score

95. Does job training on the documented procedures need to be part of the process team's education and training?
<--- Score

96. How will new or emerging customer needs/ requirements be checked/communicated to orient the process toward meeting the new specifications and continually reducing variation?
<--- Score

97. How will report readings be checked to effectively monitor performance?
<--- Score

98. Is reporting being used or needed?
<--- Score

Add up total points for this section:
_____ = Total points for this section

Divided by: _____ (number of statements answered) = _____ Average score for this section

Transfer your score to the Maintenance of software Index at the beginning of the Self-Assessment.

CRITERION #7: SUSTAIN:

INTENT: Retain the benefits.

In my belief, the answer to this question is clearly defined:

5 Strongly Agree

4 Agree

3 Neutral

2 Disagree

1 Strongly Disagree

1. How important is Maintenance of software to the user organizations mission?
<--- Score

2. What Maintenance of software modifications can you make work for you?
<--- Score

3. What is the recommended frequency of auditing?
<--- Score

4. Are new benefits received and understood?
<--- Score

5. What happens at your organization when people fail?
<--- Score

6. Do Maintenance of software rules make a reasonable demand on a users capabilities?
<--- Score

7. What counts that you are not counting?
<--- Score

8. Who are your customers?
<--- Score

9. What unique value proposition (UVP) do you offer?
<--- Score

10. How do you listen to customers to obtain actionable information?
<--- Score

11. Where can you break convention?
<--- Score

12. What is your formula for success in Maintenance of software ?
<--- Score

13. Who will provide the final approval of Maintenance of software deliverables?
<--- Score

14. What is the big Maintenance of software idea?
<--- Score

15. What are the long-term Maintenance of software goals?
<--- Score

16. Are you changing as fast as the world around you?
<--- Score

17. How do you deal with Maintenance of software changes?
<--- Score

18. How much contingency will be available in the budget?
<--- Score

19. How can you become the company that would put you out of business?
<--- Score

20. What are the short and long-term Maintenance of software goals?
<--- Score

21. Why is it important to have senior management support for a Maintenance of software project?
<--- Score

22. What management system can you use to leverage the Maintenance of software experience, ideas, and concerns of the people closest to the work to be done?
<--- Score

23. Which functions and people interact with the supplier and or customer?
<--- Score

24. In retrospect, of the projects that you pulled the plug on, what percent do you wish had been allowed to keep going, and what percent do you wish had ended earlier?
<--- Score

25. How likely is it that a customer would recommend your company to a friend or colleague?
<--- Score

26. What is a feasible sequencing of reform initiatives over time?
<--- Score

27. What would you recommend your friend do if he/she were facing this dilemma?
<--- Score

28. What knowledge, skills and characteristics mark a good Maintenance of software project manager?
<--- Score

29. How does Maintenance of software integrate with other stakeholder initiatives?
<--- Score

30. Who are four people whose careers you have enhanced?
<--- Score

31. Who do you think the world wants your

organization to be?
<--- Score

32. How do you assess the Maintenance of software pitfalls that are inherent in implementing it?
<--- Score

33. If you got fired and a new hire took your place, what would she do different?
<--- Score

34. Ask yourself: how would you do this work if you only had one staff member to do it?
<--- Score

35. What are the usability implications of Maintenance of software actions?
<--- Score

36. How do you manage Maintenance of software Knowledge Management (KM)?
<--- Score

37. Do you feel that more should be done in the Maintenance of software area?
<--- Score

38. What must you excel at?
<--- Score

39. How are you doing compared to your industry?
<--- Score

40. Why is Maintenance of software important for you now?
<--- Score

41. Which models, tools and techniques are necessary?
<--- Score

42. Which individuals, teams or departments will be involved in Maintenance of software?
<--- Score

43. Are you satisfied with your current role? If not, what is missing from it?
<--- Score

44. Is a Maintenance of software breakthrough on the horizon?
<--- Score

45. What stupid rule would you most like to kill?
<--- Score

46. What are the rules and assumptions your industry operates under? What if the opposite were true?
<--- Score

47. When information truly is ubiquitous, when reach and connectivity are completely global, when computing resources are infinite, and when a whole new set of impossibilities are not only possible, but happening, what will that do to your business?
<--- Score

48. What would have to be true for the option on the table to be the best possible choice?
<--- Score

49. Who will determine interim and final deadlines?

<--- Score

50. What is your competitive advantage?
<--- Score

51. Are there any activities that you can take off your to do list?
<--- Score

52. What are the business goals Maintenance of software is aiming to achieve?
<--- Score

53. Who do you want your customers to become?
<--- Score

54. Who have you, as a company, historically been when you've been at your best?
<--- Score

55. How do you determine the key elements that affect Maintenance of software workforce satisfaction, how are these elements determined for different workforce groups and segments?
<--- Score

56. Will there be any necessary staff changes (redundancies or new hires)?
<--- Score

57. How do you create buy-in?
<--- Score

58. Is Maintenance of software realistic, or are you setting yourself up for failure?
<--- Score

59. Think of your Maintenance of software project, what are the main functions?
<--- Score

60. How do you proactively clarify deliverables and Maintenance of software quality expectations?
<--- Score

61. Were lessons learned captured and communicated?
<--- Score

62. How do you provide a safe environment -physically and emotionally?
<--- Score

63. Is there a work around that you can use?
<--- Score

64. Is Maintenance of software dependent on the successful delivery of a current project?
<--- Score

65. Are you making progress, and are you making progress as Maintenance of software leaders?
<--- Score

66. How do you track customer value, profitability or financial return, organizational success, and sustainability?
<--- Score

67. Has implementation been effective in reaching specified objectives so far?
<--- Score

68. If you had to rebuild your organization without any traditional competitive advantages (i.e., no killer technology, promising research, innovative product/ service delivery model, etcetera), how would your people have to approach their work and collaborate together in order to create the necessary conditions for success?
<--- Score

69. Can you do all this work?
<--- Score

70. What did you miss in the interview for the worst hire you ever made?
<--- Score

71. If there were zero limitations, what would you do differently?
<--- Score

72. Marketing budgets are tighter, consumers are more skeptical, and social media has changed forever the way we talk about Maintenance of software, how do you gain traction?
<--- Score

73. How do you cross-sell and up-sell your Maintenance of software success?
<--- Score

74. What are internal and external Maintenance of software relations?
<--- Score

75. How do you foster the skills, knowledge, talents,

attributes, and characteristics you want to have?
<--- Score

76. Which Maintenance of software goals are the most important?
<--- Score

77. How is implementation research currently incorporated into each of your goals?
<--- Score

78. What you are going to do to affect the numbers?
<--- Score

79. What threat is Maintenance of software addressing?
<--- Score

80. How do you accomplish your long range Maintenance of software goals?
<--- Score

81. Are all key stakeholders present at all Structured Walkthroughs?
<--- Score

82. What one word do you want to own in the minds of your customers, employees, and partners?
<--- Score

83. What trophy do you want on your mantle?
<--- Score

84. Who else should you help?

<--- Score

85. What are the gaps in your knowledge and experience?
<--- Score

86. How long will it take to change?
<--- Score

87. Are you maintaining a past–present–future perspective throughout the Maintenance of software discussion?
<--- Score

88. Is a Maintenance of software team work effort in place?
<--- Score

89. How will you insure seamless interoperability of Maintenance of software moving forward?
<--- Score

90. Do you know who is a friend or a foe?
<--- Score

91. What are your personal philosophies regarding Maintenance of software and how do they influence your work?
<--- Score

92. How do you foster innovation?
<--- Score

93. Why should you adopt a Maintenance of software framework?
<--- Score

94. If you had to leave your organization for a year and the only communication you could have with employees/colleagues was a single paragraph, what would you write?
<--- Score

95. Have new benefits been realized?
<--- Score

96. What have been your experiences in defining long range Maintenance of software goals?
<--- Score

97. How do you stay inspired?
<--- Score

98. If you weren't already in this business, would you enter it today? And if not, what are you going to do about it?
<--- Score

99. How can you negotiate Maintenance of software successfully with a stubborn boss, an irate client, or a deceitful coworker?
<--- Score

100. Whom among your colleagues do you trust, and for what?
<--- Score

101. Did your employees make progress today?
<--- Score

102. What does your signature ensure?
<--- Score

103. What is the kind of project structure that would be appropriate for your Maintenance of software project, should it be formal and complex, or can it be less formal and relatively simple?
<--- Score

104. What new services of functionality will be implemented next with Maintenance of software ?
<--- Score

105. Who is responsible for Maintenance of software?
<--- Score

106. What business benefits will Maintenance of software goals deliver if achieved?
<--- Score

107. Instead of going to current contacts for new ideas, what if you reconnected with dormant contacts--the people you used to know? If you were going reactivate a dormant tie, who would it be?
<--- Score

108. Will it be accepted by users?
<--- Score

109. Are the assumptions believable and achievable?
<--- Score

110. What are the challenges?
<--- Score

111. What is something you believe that nearly no one agrees with you on?

<--- Score

112. Are assumptions made in Maintenance of software stated explicitly?
<--- Score

113. Who is responsible for errors?
<--- Score

114. How do customers see your organization?
<--- Score

115. Why not do Maintenance of software?
<--- Score

116. Is your strategy driving your strategy? Or is the way in which you allocate resources driving your strategy?
<--- Score

117. Why should people listen to you?
<--- Score

118. Do you have past Maintenance of software successes?
<--- Score

119. If no one would ever find out about your accomplishments, how would you lead differently?
<--- Score

120. How do you keep records, of what?
<--- Score

121. Is the Maintenance of software organization completing tasks effectively and efficiently?

<--- Score

122. If you were responsible for initiating and implementing major changes in your organization, what steps might you take to ensure acceptance of those changes?
<--- Score

123. What will be the consequences to the stakeholder (financial, reputation etc) if Maintenance of software does not go ahead or fails to deliver the objectives?
<--- Score

124. What role does communication play in the success or failure of a Maintenance of software project?
<--- Score

125. What happens if you do not have enough funding?
<--- Score

126. How do you ensure that implementations of Maintenance of software products are done in a way that ensures safety?
<--- Score

127. Can the schedule be done in the given time?
<--- Score

128. Are you paying enough attention to the partners your company depends on to succeed?
<--- Score

129. How do senior leaders deploy your organizations

vision and values through your leadership system, to the workforce, to key suppliers and partners, and to customers and other stakeholders, as appropriate?
<--- Score

130. Do you have enough freaky customers in your portfolio pushing you to the limit day in and day out?
<--- Score

131. Who is the main stakeholder, with ultimate responsibility for driving Maintenance of software forward?
<--- Score

132. If your company went out of business tomorrow, would anyone who doesn't get a paycheck here care?
<--- Score

133. If you find that you havent accomplished one of the goals for one of the steps of the Maintenance of software strategy, what will you do to fix it?
<--- Score

134. Would you rather sell to knowledgeable and informed customers or to uninformed customers?
<--- Score

135. What trouble can you get into?
<--- Score

136. Why do and why don't your customers like your organization?
<--- Score

137. What is it like to work for you?
<--- Score

138. Who will be responsible for deciding whether Maintenance of software goes ahead or not after the initial investigations?

<--- Score

139. What are the top 3 things at the forefront of your Maintenance of software agendas for the next 3 years?

<--- Score

140. Are you / should you be revolutionary or evolutionary?

<--- Score

141. What may be the consequences for the performance of an organization if all stakeholders are not consulted regarding Maintenance of software?

<--- Score

142. Why will customers want to buy your organizations products/services?

<--- Score

143. In a project to restructure Maintenance of software outcomes, which stakeholders would you involve?

<--- Score

144. How do you engage the workforce, in addition to satisfying them?

<--- Score

145. How will you know that the Maintenance of software project has been successful?

<--- Score

146. At what moment would you think; Will I get fired?
<--- Score

147. What is the source of the strategies for Maintenance of software strengthening and reform?
<--- Score

148. If your customer were your grandmother, would you tell her to buy what you're selling?
<--- Score

149. Do you say no to customers for no reason?
<--- Score

150. Is the impact that Maintenance of software has shown?
<--- Score

151. What are specific Maintenance of software rules to follow?
<--- Score

152. What are the success criteria that will indicate that Maintenance of software objectives have been met and the benefits delivered?
<--- Score

153. Can you maintain your growth without detracting from the factors that have contributed to your success?
<--- Score

154. Who, on the executive team or the board, has spoken to a customer recently?
<--- Score

155. What are your most important goals for the strategic Maintenance of software objectives?
<--- Score

156. Are the criteria for selecting recommendations stated?
<--- Score

157. How do you set Maintenance of software stretch targets and how do you get people to not only participate in setting these stretch targets but also that they strive to achieve these?
<--- Score

158. What is effective Maintenance of software?
<--- Score

159. Are you using a design thinking approach and integrating Innovation, Maintenance of software Experience, and Brand Value?
<--- Score

160. Is it economical; do you have the time and money?
<--- Score

161. How can you incorporate support to ensure safe and effective use of Maintenance of software into the services that you provide?
<--- Score

162. Have benefits been optimized with all key stakeholders?
<--- Score

163. To whom do you add value?
<--- Score

164. Can you break it down?
<--- Score

165. How will you motivate the stakeholders with the least vested interest?
<--- Score

166. What do we do when new problems arise?
<--- Score

167. Who do we want your customers to become?
<--- Score

168. Who will manage the integration of tools?
<--- Score

169. What is the craziest thing you can do?
<--- Score

170. How do you govern and fulfill your societal responsibilities?
<--- Score

171. What are the key enablers to make this Maintenance of software move?
<--- Score

172. What is your question? Why?
<--- Score

173. Do you have an implicit bias for capital investments over people investments?
<--- Score

174. How do you make it meaningful in connecting Maintenance of software with what users do day-to-day?

<--- Score

175. What are you challenging?

<--- Score

176. What are the potential basics of Maintenance of software fraud?

<--- Score

177. Is there any reason to believe the opposite of my current belief?

<--- Score

178. In the past year, what have you done (or could you have done) to increase the accurate perception of your company/brand as ethical and honest?

<--- Score

179. What is the purpose of Maintenance of software in relation to the mission?

<--- Score

180. Is there any existing Maintenance of software governance structure?

<--- Score

181. How do you go about securing Maintenance of software?

<--- Score

182. What was the last experiment you ran?

<--- Score

183. Who uses your product in ways you never expected?
<--- Score

184. What is the range of capabilities?
<--- Score

185. How do you know if you are successful?
<--- Score

186. What is the funding source for this project?
<--- Score

187. What Maintenance of software skills are most important?
<--- Score

188. What is the overall talent health of your organization as a whole at senior levels, and for each organization reporting to a member of the Senior Leadership Team?
<--- Score

189. How can you become more high-tech but still be high touch?
<--- Score

190. What are strategies for increasing support and reducing opposition?
<--- Score

191. Who is on the team?
<--- Score

192. How do you lead with Maintenance of software

in mind?
<--- Score

193. Is your basic point _____ or _____?
<--- Score

194. Are your responses positive or negative?
<--- Score

195. Do you have the right people on the bus?
<--- Score

196. Do you have the right capabilities and capacities?
<--- Score

197. What potential megatrends could make your business model obsolete?
<--- Score

198. How do you keep the momentum going?
<--- Score

199. How do you transition from the baseline to the target?
<--- Score

200. Do you think Maintenance of software accomplishes the goals you expect it to accomplish?
<--- Score

201. What are the essentials of internal Maintenance of software management?
<--- Score

202. What is an unauthorized commitment?

<--- Score

203. What have you done to protect your business from competitive encroachment?
<--- Score

204. Do you see more potential in people than they do in themselves?
<--- Score

205. What projects are going on in the organization today, and what resources are those projects using from the resource pools?
<--- Score

206. Political -is anyone trying to undermine this project?
<--- Score

207. What could happen if you do not do it?
<--- Score

208. Whose voice (department, ethnic group, women, older workers, etc) might you have missed hearing from in your company, and how might you amplify this voice to create positive momentum for your business?
<--- Score

209. What are current Maintenance of software paradigms?
<--- Score

210. What should you stop doing?
<--- Score

211. If you do not follow, then how to lead?
<--- Score

212. Do you think you know, or do you know you know ?
<--- Score

Add up total points for this section:
_ _ _ _ _ = Total points for this section

Divided by: _ _ _ _ _ _ (number of
statements answered) = _ _ _ _ _ _
Average score for this section

Transfer your score to the Maintenance
of software Index at the beginning of
the Self-Assessment.

Maintenance Of Software and Managing Projects, Criteria for Project Managers:

1.0 Initiating Process Group: Maintenance Of Software

1. The Maintenance Of Software project managers have maximum authority in which type of organization?

2. What is the stake of others in your Maintenance Of Software project?

3. Mitigate. what will you do to minimize the impact should the risk event occur?

4. Are the Maintenance Of Software project team and stakeholders meeting regularly and using a meeting agenda and taking notes to accurately document what is being covered and what happened in the weekly meetings?

5. Based on your Maintenance Of Software project communication management plan, what worked well?

6. What do they need to know about the Maintenance Of Software project?

7. What are the inputs required to produce the deliverables?

8. Who is funding the Maintenance Of Software project?

9. Were resources available as planned?

10. How can you make your needs known?

11. How is each deliverable reviewed, verified, and validated?

12. Have the stakeholders identified all individual requirements pertaining to business process?

13. Although the Maintenance Of Software project manager does not directly manage procurement and contracting activities, who does manage procurement and contracting activities in your organization then if not the PM?

14. The process to Manage Stakeholders is part of which process group?

15. Are you certain deliverables are properly completed and meet quality standards?

16. What were things that you need to improve?

17. Specific - is the objective clear in terms of what, how, when, and where the situation will be changed?

18. What are the constraints?

19. What were the challenges that you encountered during the execution of a previous Maintenance Of Software project that you would not want to repeat?

20. If the risk event occurs, what will you do?

1.1 Project Charter: Maintenance Of Software

21. Review the general mission What system will be affected by the improvement efforts?

22. Maintenance Of Software project deliverables: what is the Maintenance Of Software project going to produce?

23. When is a charter needed?

24. What outcome, in measureable terms, are you hoping to accomplish?

25. How much?

26. What is the most common tool for helping define the detail?

27. What is the justification?

28. How are Maintenance Of Software projects different from operations?

29. What are the known stakeholder requirements?

30. How will you know that a change is an improvement?

31. For whom?

32. Will this replace an existing product?

33. How will you learn more about the process or system you are trying to improve?

34. What are you striving to accomplish (measurable goal(s))?

35. Major high-level milestone targets: what events measure progress?

36. How will you know a change is an improvement?

37. Who is the sponsor?

38. Where and how does the team fit within your organization structure?

39. Success determination factors: how will the success of the Maintenance Of Software project be determined from the customers perspective?

40. What are the deliverables?

1.2 Stakeholder Register: Maintenance Of Software

41. What opportunities exist to provide communications?

42. Who wants to talk about Security?

43. What is the power of the stakeholder?

44. How will reports be created?

45. How much influence do they have on the Maintenance Of Software project?

46. Who is managing stakeholder engagement?

47. What & Why?

48. Who are the stakeholders?

49. Is your organization ready for change?

50. How big is the gap?

51. How should employers make voices heard?

52. What are the major Maintenance Of Software project milestones requiring communications or providing communications opportunities?

1.3 Stakeholder Analysis Matrix: Maintenance Of Software

53. Beneficiaries; who are the potential beneficiaries?

54. Which conditions out of the control of the management are crucial for the achievement of the outputs?

55. Sustainable financial backing?

56. Are they likely to influence the success or failure of your Maintenance Of Software project?

57. Which conditions out of the control of the management are crucial to contribute for the achievement of the development objective?

58. Competitors vulnerabilities?

59. Do the stakeholders goals and expectations support or conflict with the Maintenance Of Software project goals?

60. Location and geographical?

61. Usps (unique selling points)?

62. Do recommendations include actions to address any differential distribution of impacts?

63. Volumes, production, economies?

64. Disadvantages of proposition?

65. What organizational arrangements are planned to ensure the Maintenance Of Software project achieves its social development outcomes?

66. Who can contribute financial or technical resources towards the work?

67. Who has been involved in the area (thematic or geographic) in the past?

68. Who determines value?

69. Why do you need to manage Maintenance Of Software project Risk?

70. What can the stakeholder prevent from happening?

71. Who is most interested in information about the topic and/or has previously initiated interest?

72. What is the relationship among stakeholders?

2.0 Planning Process Group: Maintenance Of Software

73. Are work methodologies, financial instruments, etc. shared among departments, organizations and Maintenance Of Software projects?

74. What types of differentiated effects are resulting from the Maintenance Of Software project and to what extent?

75. To what extent do the intervention objectives and strategies of the Maintenance Of Software project respond to your organizations plans?

76. What is the critical path for this Maintenance Of Software project, and what is the duration of the critical path?

77. How are it Maintenance Of Software projects different?

78. In what ways can the governance of the Maintenance Of Software project be improved so that it has greater likelihood of achieving future sustainability?

79. You did your readings, yes?

80. Who are the Maintenance Of Software project stakeholders?

81. Will the products created live up to the necessary

quality?

82. You are creating your WBS and find that you keep decomposing tasks into smaller and smaller units. How can you tell when you are done?

83. What is the difference between the early schedule and late schedule?

84. What is the NEXT thing to do?

85. What type of estimation method are you using?

86. Why do it Maintenance Of Software projects fail?

87. Contingency planning. if a risk event occurs, what will you do?

88. To what extent have the target population and participants made the activities own, taking an active role in it?

89. If you are late, will anybody notice?

90. What input will you be required to provide the Maintenance Of Software project team?

91. What do they need to know about the Maintenance Of Software project?

92. How can you tell when you are done?

2.1 Project Management Plan: Maintenance Of Software

93. Are the existing and future without-plan conditions reasonable and appropriate?

94. Are there non-structural buyout or relocation recommendations?

95. How do you organize the costs in the Maintenance Of Software project management plan?

96. How do you manage time?

97. Where does all this information come from?

98. Why Change?

99. What goes into your Maintenance Of Software project Charter?

100. Has the selected plan been formulated using cost effectiveness and incremental analysis techniques?

101. How do you manage integration?

102. Are alternatives safe, functional, constructible, economical, reasonable and sustainable?

103. Are there any Client staffing expectations?

104. What are the training needs?

105. If the Maintenance Of Software project is complex or scope is specialized, do you have appropriate and/or qualified staff available to perform the tasks?

106. Are the proposed Maintenance Of Software project purposes different than a previously authorized Maintenance Of Software project?

107. Who manages integration?

108. Is there an incremental analysis/cost effectiveness analysis of proposed mitigation features based on an approved method and using an accepted model?

109. What is risk management?

110. Are comparable cost estimates used for comparing, screening and selecting alternative plans, and has a reasonable cost estimate been developed for the recommended plan?

2.2 Scope Management Plan: Maintenance Of Software

111. Cost / benefit analysis?

112. Is there an onboarding process in place?

113. Do Maintenance Of Software project teams & team members report on status / activities / progress?

114. Do you secure formal approval of changes and requirements from stakeholders?

115. Is stakeholder involvement adequate?

116. How much money have you spent?

117. What problem is being solved by delivering this Maintenance Of Software project?

118. Organizational unit (e.g., department, team, or person) who will accept responsibility for satisfactory completion of the item?

119. Are action items captured and managed?

120. Is each item clearly and completely defined?

121. Are calculations and results of analyzes essentially correct?

122. Is the Maintenance Of Software project status reviewed with the steering and executive teams at

appropriate intervals?

123. Can the Maintenance Of Software project team do several activities in parallel?

124. Are you spending the right amount of money for specific tasks?

125. How relevant is this attribute to this Maintenance Of Software project or audit?

126. What went right?

127. Is an industry recognized mechanized support tool(s) being used for Maintenance Of Software project scheduling & tracking?

128. What are the risks that could significantly affect the schedule of the Maintenance Of Software project?

129. Have activity relationships and interdependencies within tasks been adequately identified?

130. What are the acceptance criteria (process and criteria to be met for key stakeholder acceptance) and who is authorized to sign off?

2.3 Requirements Management Plan: Maintenance Of Software

131. Do you know which stakeholders will participate in the requirements effort?

132. Is any organizational data being used or stored?

133. Who will perform the analysis?

134. Have stakeholders been instructed in the Change Control process?

135. Controlling Maintenance Of Software project requirements involves monitoring the status of the Maintenance Of Software project requirements and managing changes to the requirements. Who is responsible for monitoring and tracking the Maintenance Of Software project requirements?

136. The wbs is developed as part of a joint planning session. and how do you know that youhave done this right?

137. Did you use declarative statements?

138. Who is responsible for monitoring and tracking the Maintenance Of Software project requirements?

139. Who will approve the requirements (and if multiple approvers, in what order)?

140. Do you have an agreed upon process for alerting

the Maintenance Of Software project Manager if a request for change in requirements leads to a product scope change?

141. Is infrastructure setup part of your Maintenance Of Software project?

142. After the requirements are gathered and set forth on the requirements register, theyre little more than a laundry list of items. Some may be duplicates, some might conflict with others and some will be too broad or too vague to understand. Describe how the requirements will be analyzed. Who will perform the analysis?

143. What performance metrics will be used?

144. Is there formal agreement on who has authority to request a change in requirements?

145. How will the requirements become prioritized?

146. Will the contractors involved take full responsibility?

147. How will bidders price evaluations be done, by deliverables, phases, or in a big bang?

148. Will you use an assessment of the Maintenance Of Software project environment as a tool to discover risk to the requirements process?

149. Who will finally present the work or product(s) for acceptance?

2.4 Requirements Documentation: Maintenance Of Software

150. Is the requirement properly understood?

151. Is new technology needed?

152. Does your organization restrict technical alternatives?

153. What marketing channels do you want to use: e-mail, letter or sms?

154. Can the requirements be checked?

155. What are the potential disadvantages/ advantages?

156. Are there legal issues?

157. Where do you define what is a customer, what are the attributes of customer?

158. Do technical resources exist?

159. Who provides requirements?

160. What variations exist for a process?

161. Consistency. are there any requirements conflicts?

162. Verifiability. can the requirements be checked?

163. What happens when requirements are wrong?

164. What kind of entity is a problem ?

165. What will be the integration problems?

166. How does what is being described meet the business need?

167. What are the acceptance criteria?

168. How do you get the user to tell you what they want?

169. The problem with gathering requirements is right there in the word gathering. What images does it conjure?

2.5 Requirements Traceability Matrix: Maintenance Of Software

170. Is there a requirements traceability process in place?

171. How do you manage scope?

172. Describe the process for approving requirements so they can be added to the traceability matrix and Maintenance Of Software project work can be performed. Will the Maintenance Of Software project requirements become approved in writing?

173. How small is small enough?

174. What is the WBS?

175. What are the chronologies, contingencies, consequences, criteria?

176. Why do you manage scope?

177. What percentage of Maintenance Of Software projects are producing traceability matrices between requirements and other work products?

178. How will it affect the stakeholders personally in career?

179. Do you have a clear understanding of all subcontracts in place?

180. Will you use a Requirements Traceability Matrix?

181. Why use a WBS?

2.6 Project Scope Statement: Maintenance Of Software

182. Will this process be communicated to the customer and Maintenance Of Software project team?

183. Has the format for tracking and monitoring schedules and costs been defined?

184. Does the scope statement still need some clarity?

185. Is the Maintenance Of Software project manager qualified and experienced in Maintenance Of Software project management?

186. Is there a Quality Assurance Plan documented and filed?

187. Will the Maintenance Of Software project risks be managed according to the Maintenance Of Software projects risk management process?

188. Will tasks be marked complete only after QA has been successfully completed?

189. Will the qa related information be reported regularly as part of the status reporting mechanisms?

190. Identify how your team and you will create the Maintenance Of Software project scope statement and the work breakdown structure (WBS). Document how you will create the Maintenance Of Software project scope statement and WBS, and make sure

you answer the following questions: In defining Maintenance Of Software project scope and the WBS, will you and your Maintenance Of Software project team be using methods defined by your organization, methods defined by the Maintenance Of Software project management office (PMO), or other methods?

191. If there is an independent oversight contractor, have they signed off on the Maintenance Of Software project Plan?

192. Are there issues that could affect the existing requirements for the result, service, or product if the scope changes?

193. Have you been able to thoroughly document the Maintenance Of Software projects assumptions and constraints?

194. Is there an information system for the Maintenance Of Software project?

195. Is your organization structure appropriate for the Maintenance Of Software projects size and complexity?

196. Have the configuration management functions been assigned?

197. Will an issue form be in use?

198. What is a process you might recommend to verify the accuracy of the research deliverable?

199. What is the product of this Maintenance Of Software project?

200. How often do you estimate that the scope might change, and why?

201. What went wrong?

2.7 Assumption and Constraint Log: Maintenance Of Software

202. What strengths do you have?

203. Do you know what your customers expectations are regarding this process?

204. Should factors be unpredictable over time?

205. Have all stakeholders been identified?

206. Are best practices and metrics employed to identify issues, progress, performance, etc.?

207. How relevant is this attribute to this Maintenance Of Software project or audit?

208. Are there processes in place to ensure internal consistency between the source code components?

209. Is the process working, and people are not executing in compliance of the process?

210. Security analysis has access to information that is sanitized?

211. Are there procedures in place to effectively manage interdependencies with other Maintenance Of Software projects / systems?

212. Does a documented Maintenance Of Software project organizational policy & plan (i.e. governance

model) exist?

213. Contradictory information between document sections?

214. What threats might prevent you from getting there?

215. What do you audit?

216. Are formal code reviews conducted?

217. Do the requirements meet the standards of correctness, completeness, consistency, accuracy, and readability?

218. What to do at recovery?

219. Have the scope, objectives, costs, benefits and impacts been communicated to all involved and/or impacted stakeholders and work groups?

220. Are there processes defining how software will be developed including development methods, overall timeline for development, software product standards, and traceability?

221. How do you design an auditing system?

2.8 Work Breakdown Structure: Maintenance Of Software

222. What is the probability that the Maintenance Of Software project duration will exceed xx weeks?

223. How many levels?

224. When would you develop a Work Breakdown Structure?

225. Do you need another level?

226. Why is it useful?

227. When do you stop?

228. When does it have to be done?

229. What is the probability of completing the Maintenance Of Software project in less that xx days?

230. Where does it take place?

231. Is it still viable?

232. Who has to do it?

233. How much detail?

234. How big is a work-package?

235. Is it a change in scope?

236. Can you make it?

237. Is the work breakdown structure (wbs) defined and is the scope of the Maintenance Of Software project clear with assigned deliverable owners?

238. How will you and your Maintenance Of Software project team define the Maintenance Of Software projects scope and work breakdown structure?

2.9 WBS Dictionary: Maintenance Of Software

239. Are budgets or values assigned to work packages and planning packages in terms of dollars, hours, or other measurable units?

240. Does the contractors system provide for determination of price variance by comparing planned Vs actual commitments?

241. Are indirect costs charged to the appropriate indirect pools and incurring organization?

242. Is subcontracted work defined and identified to the appropriate subcontractor within the proper WBS element?

243. Are the requirements for all items of overhead established by rational, traceable processes?

244. Are current work performance indicators and goals relatable to original goals as modified by contractual changes, replanning, and reprogramming actions?

245. Software specification, development, integration, and testing, licenses ?

246. Does the contractors system identify work accomplishment against the schedule plan?

247. Are Maintenance Of Software projected

overhead costs in each pool and the associated direct costs used as the basis for establishing interim rates for allocating overhead to contracts?

248. Are direct or indirect cost adjustments being accomplished according to accounting procedures acceptable to us?

249. Is data disseminated to the contractors management timely, accurate, and usable?

250. Budgets assigned to major functional organizations?

251. Intermediate schedules, as required, which provide a logical sequence from the master schedule to the control account level?

252. Is cost performance measurement at the point in time most suitable for the category of material involved, and no earlier than the time of actual receipt of material?

253. Appropriate work authorization documents which subdivide the contractual effort and responsibilities, within functional organizations?

254. Does the contractors system include procedures for measuring the performance of critical subcontractors?

255. Identify potential or actual overruns and underruns?

256. What is the goal?

2.10 Schedule Management Plan: Maintenance Of Software

257. Is a process defined for baseline approval and control?

258. Are Maintenance Of Software project leaders committed to this Maintenance Of Software project full time?

259. Does the schedule have reasonable float?

260. Have all documents been archived in a Maintenance Of Software project repository for each release?

261. Are corrective actions and variances reported?

262. Is there an on-going process in place to monitor Maintenance Of Software project risks?

263. Is the critical path valid?

264. Is the plan consistent with industry best practices?

265. Have Maintenance Of Software project success criteria been defined?

266. Has the Maintenance Of Software project manager been identified?

267. Do Maintenance Of Software project teams &

team members report on status / activities / progress?

268. Has the business need been clearly defined?

269. Have all necessary approvals been obtained?

270. Is there a formal process for updating the Maintenance Of Software project baseline?

271. Has the Maintenance Of Software project scope been baselined?

272. Is documentation created for communication with the suppliers and Vendors?

273. Are meeting minutes captured and sent out after the meeting?

274. Is the ims used by all levels of management for Maintenance Of Software project implementation and control?

2.11 Activity List: Maintenance Of Software

275. Who will perform the work?

276. What went well?

277. What are the critical bottleneck activities?

278. Can you determine the activity that must finish, before this activity can start?

279. What is the probability the Maintenance Of Software project can be completed in xx weeks?

280. In what sequence?

281. What are you counting on?

282. When do the individual activities need to start and finish?

283. How can the Maintenance Of Software project be displayed graphically to better visualize the activities?

284. What is your organizations history in doing similar activities?

285. What is the LF and LS for each activity?

286. Is infrastructure setup part of your Maintenance Of Software project?

287. How should ongoing costs be monitored to try to keep the Maintenance Of Software project within budget?

288. Where will it be performed?

289. For other activities, how much delay can be tolerated?

290. What is the total time required to complete the Maintenance Of Software project if no delays occur?

291. How detailed should a Maintenance Of Software project get?

292. Is there anything planned that does not need to be here?

293. How will it be performed?

2.12 Activity Attributes: Maintenance Of Software

294. Where else does it apply?

295. Would you consider either of corresponding activities an outlier?

296. Can more resources be added?

297. Are the required resources available?

298. Activity: what is Missing?

299. What is missing?

300. Has management defined a definite timeframe for the turnaround or Maintenance Of Software project window?

301. Were there other ways you could have organized the data to achieve similar results?

302. Time for overtime?

303. What activity do you think you should spend the most time on?

304. How difficult will it be to complete specific activities on this Maintenance Of Software project?

305. How difficult will it be to do specific activities on this Maintenance Of Software project?

306. How many resources do you need to complete the work scope within a limit of X number of days?

307. Have you identified the Activity Leveling Priority code value on each activity?

308. How many days do you need to complete the work scope with a limit of X number of resources?

309. How else could the items be grouped?

310. Resource is assigned to?

311. Are the required resources available or need to be acquired?

2.13 Milestone List: Maintenance Of Software

312. How soon can the activity finish?

313. What background experience, skills, and strengths does the team bring to your organization?

314. Insurmountable weaknesses?

315. Vital contracts and partners?

316. New USPs?

317. What is the market for your technology, product or service?

318. Effects on core activities, distraction?

319. How will the milestone be verified?

320. How late can the activity finish?

321. Own known vulnerabilities?

322. It is to be a narrative text providing the crucial aspects of your Maintenance Of Software project proposal answering what, who, how, when and where?

323. When will the Maintenance Of Software project be complete?

324. What has been done so far?

325. What date will the task finish?

326. How late can the activity start?

327. What specific improvements did you make to the Maintenance Of Software project proposal since the previous time?

328. Do you foresee any technical risks or developmental challenges?

329. Environmental effects?

330. Competitive advantages?

2.14 Network Diagram: Maintenance Of Software

331. If the Maintenance Of Software project network diagram cannot change and you have extra personnel resources, what is the BEST thing to do?

332. What is the completion time?

333. What can be done concurrently?

334. Review the logical flow of the network diagram. Take a look at which activities you have first and then sequence the activities. Do they make sense?

335. What activities must follow this activity?

336. What job or jobs follow it?

337. Can you calculate the confidence level?

338. What controls the start and finish of a job?

339. What job or jobs precede it?

340. Exercise: what is the probability that the Maintenance Of Software project duration will exceed xx weeks?

341. If x is long, what would be the completion time if you break x into two parallel parts of y weeks and z weeks?

342. Are you on time?

343. How difficult will it be to do specific activities on this Maintenance Of Software project?

344. Why must you schedule milestones, such as reviews, throughout the Maintenance Of Software project?

345. Which type of network diagram allows you to depict four types of dependencies?

346. What job or jobs could run concurrently?

347. Planning: who, how long, what to do?

348. What must be completed before an activity can be started?

2.15 Activity Resource Requirements: Maintenance Of Software

349. How do you handle petty cash?

350. Which logical relationship does the PDM use most often?

351. When does monitoring begin?

352. How many signatures do you require on a check and does this match what is in your policy and procedures?

353. Do you use tools like decomposition and rolling-wave planning to produce the activity list and other outputs?

354. What is the Work Plan Standard?

355. Anything else?

356. Why do you do that?

357. Are there unresolved issues that need to be addressed?

358. Other support in specific areas?

359. Organizational Applicability?

360. What are constraints that you might find during the Human Resource Planning process?

2.16 Resource Breakdown Structure: Maintenance Of Software

361. Any changes from stakeholders?

362. Changes based on input from stakeholders?

363. How can this help you with team building?

364. When do they need the information?

365. What is each stakeholders desired outcome for the Maintenance Of Software project?

366. What is the difference between % Complete and % work?

367. Why do you do it?

368. What is the number one predictor of a groups productivity?

369. Which resource planning tool provides information on resource responsibility and accountability?

370. Who delivers the information?

371. What can you do to improve productivity?

372. Why is this important?

373. What is Maintenance Of Software project

communication management?

374. Goals for the Maintenance Of Software project. What is each stakeholders desired outcome for the Maintenance Of Software project?

375. Who is allowed to perform which functions?

376. What defines a successful Maintenance Of Software project?

377. Who needs what information?

2.17 Activity Duration Estimates: Maintenance Of Software

378. Is risk identification completed regularly throughout the Maintenance Of Software project?

379. On which process should team members spend the most time?

380. What are the main types of contracts if you do decide to outsource?

381. Are procedures defined for calculating cost estimates?

382. How do theories relate to Maintenance Of Software project management?

383. Which tips for taking the PMP exam do you think would be most helpful for you?

384. Does a process exist to determine the potential loss or gain if risk events occur?

385. What is pmp certification, and why do you think the number of people earning it has grown so much in the past ten years?

386. Maintenance Of Software project manager has received activity duration estimates from his team. Which does one need in order to complete schedule development?

387. Based on , if you need to shorten the duration of the Maintenance Of Software project, what activity would you try to shorten?

388. If you plan to take the PMP exam soon, what should you do to prepare?

389. Consider the examples of poor quality in information technology Maintenance Of Software projects presented in the What Went Wrong?

390. How does Maintenance Of Software project integration management relate to the Maintenance Of Software project life cycle, stakeholders, and the other Maintenance Of Software project management knowledge areas?

391. Do you think Maintenance Of Software project managers of large information technology Maintenance Of Software projects need strong technical skills?

392. How can software assist in procuring goods and services?

393. List five reasons why organizations outsource. Why is there a growing trend in outsourcing, especially in the government?

394. Explanation notice how many choices are half right?

395. How does a Maintenance Of Software project life cycle differ from a product life cycle?

396. Is training acquired to enhance the skills,

knowledge and capabilities of the Maintenance Of Software project team?

397. Are expert judgment and historical information utilized to estimate activity duration?

2.18 Duration Estimating Worksheet: Maintenance Of Software

398. What is the total time required to complete the Maintenance Of Software project if no delays occur?

399. What utility impacts are there?

400. How should ongoing costs be monitored to try to keep the Maintenance Of Software project within budget?

401. Will the Maintenance Of Software project collaborate with the local community and leverage resources?

402. Do any colleagues have experience with your organization and/or RFPs?

403. What work will be included in the Maintenance Of Software project?

404. Can the Maintenance Of Software project be constructed as planned?

405. How can the Maintenance Of Software project be displayed graphically to better visualize the activities?

406. When does your organization expect to be able to complete it?

407. Is this operation cost effective?

408. Small or large Maintenance Of Software project?

409. Why estimate costs?

410. Does the Maintenance Of Software project provide innovative ways for stakeholders to overcome obstacles or deliver better outcomes?

411. Value pocket identification & quantification what are value pockets?

412. What is your role?

413. What is an Average Maintenance Of Software project?

414. Is a construction detail attached (to aid in explanation)?

2.19 Project Schedule: Maintenance Of Software

415. Did the Maintenance Of Software project come in on schedule?

416. If you can not fix it, how do you do it differently?

417. Are quality inspections and review activities listed in the Maintenance Of Software project schedule(s)?

418. Did the final product meet or exceed user expectations?

419. Does the condition or event threaten the Maintenance Of Software projects objectives in any ways?

420. How can slack be negative?

421. How can you minimize or control changes to Maintenance Of Software project schedules?

422. Why do you need to manage Maintenance Of Software project Risk?

423. How closely did the initial Maintenance Of Software project Schedule compare with the actual schedule?

424. How do you manage Maintenance Of Software project Risk?

425. How does a Maintenance Of Software project get to be a year late ?

426. Why time management?

427. Was the Maintenance Of Software project schedule reviewed by all stakeholders and formally accepted?

428. What does that mean?

429. Meet requirements?

430. Your best shot for providing estimations how complex/how much work does the activity require?

431. Are there activities that came from a template or previous Maintenance Of Software project that are not applicable on this phase of this Maintenance Of Software project?

2.20 Cost Management Plan: Maintenance Of Software

432. Is Maintenance Of Software project status reviewed with the steering and executive teams at appropriate intervals?

433. Are all vendor contracts closed out?

434. Is it possible to track all classes of Maintenance Of Software project work (e.g. scheduled, un-scheduled, defect repair, etc.)?

435. Forecasts – how will the time and resources needed to complete the Maintenance Of Software project be forecast?

436. Have process improvement efforts been completed before requirements efforts begin?

437. Schedule preparation – how will the schedules be prepared during each phase of the Maintenance Of Software project?

438. Are post milestone Maintenance Of Software project reviews (PMPR) conducted with your organization at least once a year?

439. Cost variances – how will cost variances be identified and corrected?

440. Is pert / critical path or equivalent methodology being used?

441. Is there a formal set of procedures supporting Issues Management?

442. Are software metrics formally captured, analyzed and used as a basis for other Maintenance Of Software project estimates?

443. What weaknesses do you have?

444. Have Maintenance Of Software project team accountabilities & responsibilities been clearly defined?

445. Designated small business reserve?

446. Time management – how will the schedule impact of changes be estimated and approved?

447. Are updated Maintenance Of Software project time & resource estimates reasonable based on the current Maintenance Of Software project stage?

448. Does the Maintenance Of Software project have a Quality Culture?

449. Personnel with expertise?

450. Has your organization readiness assessment been conducted?

451. Are tasks tracked by hours?

2.21 Activity Cost Estimates: Maintenance Of Software

452. What areas were overlooked on this Maintenance Of Software project?

453. The impact and what actions were taken?

454. What is the last item a Maintenance Of Software project manager must do to finalize Maintenance Of Software project close-out?

455. Eac -estimate at completion, what is the total job expected to cost?

456. Can you delete activities or make them inactive?

457. Are cost subtotals needed?

458. What makes a good expected result statement?

459. How many activities should you have?

460. Scope statement only direct or indirect costs as well?

461. What is a Maintenance Of Software project Management Plan?

462. What defines a successful Maintenance Of Software project?

463. What happens if you cannot produce the

documentation for the single audit?

464. Is costing method consistent with study goals?

465. What cost data should be used to estimate costs during the 2-year follow-up period?

466. In which phase of the acquisition process cycle does source qualifications reside?

467. Does the activity serve a common type of customer?

468. Can you change your activities?

469. How do you treat administrative costs in the activity inventory?

470. Were you satisfied with the work?

2.22 Cost Estimating Worksheet: Maintenance Of Software

471. Ask: are others positioned to know, are others credible, and will others cooperate?

472. How will the results be shared and to whom?

473. Is it feasible to establish a control group arrangement?

474. Is the Maintenance Of Software project responsive to community need?

475. What costs are to be estimated?

476. What happens to any remaining funds not used?

477. Does the Maintenance Of Software project provide innovative ways for stakeholders to overcome obstacles or deliver better outcomes?

478. What info is needed?

479. Identify the timeframe necessary to monitor progress and collect data to determine how the selected measure has changed?

480. Can a trend be established from historical performance data on the selected measure and are the criteria for using trend analysis or forecasting methods met?

481. What can be included?

482. What additional Maintenance Of Software project(s) could be initiated as a result of this Maintenance Of Software project?

483. Will the Maintenance Of Software project collaborate with the local community and leverage resources?

484. What is the estimated labor cost today based upon this information?

485. What will others want?

486. Who is best positioned to know and assist in identifying corresponding factors?

487. What is the purpose of estimating?

2.23 Cost Baseline: Maintenance Of Software

488. Has the Maintenance Of Software project (or Maintenance Of Software project phase) been evaluated against each objective established in the product description and Integrated Maintenance Of Software project Plan?

489. What would the life cycle costs be?

490. Why do you manage cost?

491. Does a process exist for establishing a cost baseline to measure Maintenance Of Software project performance?

492. Maintenance Of Software project goals -should others be reconsidered?

493. What is the consequence?

494. Does the suggested change request seem to represent a necessary enhancement to the product?

495. How concrete were original objectives?

496. How accurate do cost estimates need to be?

497. Will the Maintenance Of Software project fail if the change request is not executed?

498. Definition of done can be traced back to the

definitions of what are you providing to the customer in terms of deliverables?

499. At which frequency ?

500. What is it ?

501. Has the Maintenance Of Software project documentation been archived or otherwise disposed as described in the Maintenance Of Software project communication plan?

502. Have you identified skills that are missing from your team?

503. How likely is it to go wrong?

504. Are you asking management for something as a result of this update?

505. Is the requested change request a result of changes in other Maintenance Of Software project(s)?

2.24 Quality Management Plan: Maintenance Of Software

506. Does the plan conform to standards?

507. Have all involved stakeholders and work groups committed to the Maintenance Of Software project?

508. Who needs a qmp?

509. No superfluous information or marketing narrative?

510. How are calibration records kept?

511. How does your organization manage work to promote cooperation, individual initiative, innovation, flexibility, communications, and knowledge/skill sharing across work units?

512. How do you ensure that protocols are up to date?

513. What methods are used?

514. How do senior leaders review organizational performance?

515. What are the established criteria that sampling / testing data are compared against?

516. Does a documented Maintenance Of Software project organizational policy & plan (i.e. governance model) exist?

517. How do you decide what information to record?

518. How does your organization address regulatory, legal, and ethical compliance?

519. How are changes approved?

520. What are you trying to accomplish?

521. Are there trends or hot spots?

522. How do senior leaders create your organizational focus on customers and other stakeholders?

523. How are corresponding standards measured?

2.25 Quality Metrics: Maintenance Of Software

524. What forces exist that would cause them to change?

525. How does one achieve stability?

526. Filter visualizations of interest?

527. Are documents on hand to provide explanations of privacy and confidentiality?

528. How is it being measured?

529. Subjective quality component: customer satisfaction, how do you measure it?

530. How should customers provide input?

531. Has it met internal or external standards?

532. How do you calculate such metrics?

533. What documentation is required?

534. How effective are your security tests?

535. Was the overall quality better or worse than previous products?

536. How can the effectiveness of each of the activities be measured?

537. If the defect rate during testing is substantially higher than that of the previous release (or a similar product), then ask: Did you plan for and actually improve testing effectiveness?

538. Have alternatives been defined in the event that failure occurs?

539. What are your organizations next steps?

540. What percentage are outcome-based?

541. How exactly do you define when differences exist?

542. Is material complete (and does it meet the standards)?

543. Why is now the time for quality metrics?

2.26 Process Improvement Plan: Maintenance Of Software

544. Are you making progress on the goals?

545. To elicit goal statements, do you ask a question such as, What do you want to achieve?

546. Have the supporting tools been developed or acquired?

547. Where are you now?

548. Does your process ensure quality?

549. Why quality management?

550. What is quality and how will you ensure it?

551. Does explicit definition of the measures exist?

552. What is the return on investment?

553. Management commitment at all levels?

554. What makes people good SPI coaches?

555. How do you measure?

556. The motive is determined by asking, Why do you want to achieve this goal?

557. What personnel are the champions for the

initiative?

558. Are there forms and procedures to collect and record the data?

559. Has the time line required to move measurement results from the points of collection to databases or users been established?

560. Have storage and access mechanisms and procedures been determined?

561. If a process improvement framework is being used, which elements will help the problems and goals listed?

562. Purpose of goal: the motive is determined by asking, why do you want to achieve this goal?

563. What actions are needed to address the problems and achieve the goals?

2.27 Responsibility Assignment Matrix: Maintenance Of Software

564. Past experience – the person or the group worked at something similar in the past?

565. How do you manage human resources?

566. Performance to date and material commitment?

567. The staff characteristics – is the group or the person capable to work together as a team?

568. What are some important Maintenance Of Software project communications management tools?

569. Is the anticipated (firm and potential) business base Maintenance Of Software projected in a rational, consistent manner?

570. Detailed schedules which support control account and work package start and completion dates/events?

571. Can the contractor substantiate work package and planning package budgets?

572. Availability – will the group or the person be available within the necessary time interval?

573. Are the bases and rates for allocating costs from each indirect pool consistently applied?

574. Are material costs reported within the same period as that in which BCWP is earned for that material?

575. What does wbs accomplish?

576. What is the business need?

577. Identify potential or actual budget-based and time-based schedule variances?

578. What will the work cost?

2.28 Roles and Responsibilities: Maintenance Of Software

579. Do the values and practices inherent in the culture of your organization foster or hinder the process?

580. What expectations were NOT met?

581. What should you highlight for improvement?

582. Required skills, knowledge, experience?

583. Who is responsible for implementation activities and where will the functions, roles and responsibilities be defined?

584. Implementation of actions: Who are the responsible units?

585. What areas would you highlight for changes or improvements?

586. Are governance roles and responsibilities documented?

587. What are your major roles and responsibilities in the area of performance measurement and assessment?

588. Is there a training program in place for stakeholders covering expectations, roles and responsibilities and any addition knowledge others

need to be good stakeholders?

589. Who: who is involved?

590. Where are you most strong as a supervisor?

591. What specific behaviors did you observe?

592. Was the expectation clearly communicated?

593. Do you take the time to clearly define roles and responsibilities on Maintenance Of Software project tasks?

594. What is working well within your organizations performance management system?

595. Is feedback clearly communicated and non-judgmental?

596. What should you do now to prepare yourself for a promotion, increased responsibilities or a different job?

597. What is working well?

598. Once the responsibilities are defined for the Maintenance Of Software project, have the deliverables, roles and responsibilities been clearly communicated to every participant?

2.29 Human Resource Management Plan: Maintenance Of Software

599. Are enough systems & user personnel assigned to the Maintenance Of Software project?

600. Is your organization heading towards expansion, outsourcing of certain talents or making cut-backs to save money?

601. Are Maintenance Of Software project contact logs kept up to date?

602. Sensitivity analysis?

603. Is a payment system in place with proper reviews and approvals?

604. Are updated Maintenance Of Software project time & resource estimates reasonable based on the current Maintenance Of Software project stage?

605. Is there a set of procedures to capture, analyze and act on quality metrics?

606. Who are the people that make up your organization and whom create the success that your organization enjoys as a whole?

607. Have all team members been part of identifying risks?

608. Is this Maintenance Of Software project carried

out in partnership with other groups/organizations?

609. What are the Staffing Requirements?

610. Are the schedule estimates reasonable given the Maintenance Of Software project?

611. Are milestone deliverables effectively tracked and compared to Maintenance Of Software project plan?

612. Are actuals compared against estimates to analyze and correct variances?

613. Is your organization human?

614. Is there an approved case?

615. Is there a formal set of procedures supporting Stakeholder Management?

616. Have all involved Maintenance Of Software project stakeholders and work groups committed to the Maintenance Of Software project?

617. Does the Maintenance Of Software project have a Statement of Work?

618. Where is your organization headed?

2.30 Communications Management Plan: Maintenance Of Software

619. What is the stakeholders level of authority?

620. Who will use or be affected by the result of a Maintenance Of Software project?

621. Will messages be directly related to the release strategy or phases of the Maintenance Of Software project?

622. Can you think of other people who might have concerns or interests?

623. Are you constantly rushing from meeting to meeting?

624. What to know?

625. Why is stakeholder engagement important?

626. Who is involved as you identify stakeholders?

627. What approaches do you use?

628. Who are the members of the governing body?

629. Who to share with?

630. How often do you engage with stakeholders?

631. What does the stakeholder need from the team?

632. Who were proponents/opponents?

633. Timing: when do the effects of the communication take place?

634. Is there an important stakeholder who is actively opposed and will not receive messages?

635. How is this initiative related to other portfolios, programs, or Maintenance Of Software projects?

636. Do you ask; can you recommend others for you to talk with about this initiative?

637. Do you prepare stakeholder engagement plans?

638. How will the person responsible for executing the communication item be notified?

2.31 Risk Management Plan: Maintenance Of Software

639. Maximize short-term return on investment?

640. Which risks should get the attention?

641. What should be done with non-critical risks?

642. Are there risks to human health or the environment that need to be controlled or mitigated?

643. Do you manage the process through use of metrics?

644. Can you stabilize dynamic risk factors?

645. Prioritized components/features?

646. How is risk response planning performed?

647. Market risk -will the new service or product be useful to your organization or marketable to others?

648. Anticipated volatility of the requirements?

649. How do you manage Maintenance Of Software project Risk?

650. Number of users of the product?

651. What are the cost, schedule and resource impacts if the risk does occur?

652. How quickly does this item need to be resolved?

653. How is the audit profession changing?

654. What risks are tracked?

655. Are you on schedule?

656. How is implementation of risk actions performed?

657. Who should be notified of the occurrence of each of the indicators?

2.32 Risk Register: Maintenance Of Software

658. Risk probability and impact: how will the probabilities and impacts of risk items be assessed?

659. What action, if any, has been taken to respond to the risk?

660. When will it happen?

661. What is the probability and impact of the risk occurring?

662. Having taken action, how did the responses effect change, and where is the Maintenance Of Software project now?

663. Are there any gaps in the evidence?

664. What should you do when?

665. Severity Prediction?

666. What has changed since the last period?

667. Cost/benefit – how much will the proposed mitigations cost and how does this cost compare with the potential cost of the risk event/situation should it occur?

668. User involvement: do you have the right users?

669. Recovery actions - planned actions taken once a risk has occurred to allow you to move on. What should you do after?

670. What is a Community Risk Register?

671. Have other controls and solutions been implemented in other services which could be applied as an alternative to additional funding?

672. Who needs to know about this?

673. What could prevent you delivering on the strategic program objectives and what is being done to mitigate corresponding issues?

674. Which key risks have ineffective responses or outstanding improvement actions?

675. Amongst the action plans and recommendations that you have to introduce are there some that could stop or delay the overall program?

676. What are you going to do to limit the Maintenance Of Software projects risk exposure due to the identified risks?

2.33 Probability and Impact Assessment: Maintenance Of Software

677. What are the probabilities of chosen technologies being suitable for local conditions?

678. Costs associated with late delivery or a defective product?

679. What is the likelihood?

680. Are the facilities, expertise, resources, and management know-how available to handle the situation?

681. What things are likely to change?

682. Mitigation -how can you avoid the risk?

683. Is security a central objective?

684. Have top software and customer managers formally committed to support the Maintenance Of Software project?

685. Does the Maintenance Of Software project team have experience with the technology to be implemented?

686. What is the likelihood of a breakthrough?

687. Are the risk data complete?

688. What should be the gestation period for the Maintenance Of Software project with specific technology?

689. How are the local factors going to affect the absorption?

690. What is the probability of the risk occurring?

691. Can you avoid altogether some things that might go wrong?

692. Your customers business requirements have suddenly shifted because of a new regulatory statute, what now?

693. Are staff committed for the duration of the Maintenance Of Software project?

694. What are the current demands of the customer?

695. Should the risk be taken at all?

696. What are its business ethics?

2.34 Probability and Impact Matrix: Maintenance Of Software

697. Have customers been involved fully in the definition of requirements?

698. Lay ground work for future returns?

699. Can the Maintenance Of Software project proceed without assuming the risk?

700. What are the methods to deal with risks?

701. Have you worked with the customer in the past?

702. To what extent is the chosen technology maturing?

703. How are you working with risks?

704. What would be the best solution?

705. What are the current or emerging trends of culture?

706. What can possibly go wrong?

707. Are people attending meetings and doing work?

708. How do you analyze the risks in the different types of Maintenance Of Software projects?

709. Has something like this been done before?

710. How to prioritize risks?

711. Are compilers and code generators available and suitable for the product to be built?

712. What is the risk appetite?

713. What will the damage be?

714. Who is going to be the consortium leader?

2.35 Risk Data Sheet: Maintenance Of Software

715. What are you trying to achieve (Objectives)?

716. What will be the consequences if it happens?

717. Has the most cost-effective solution been chosen?

718. What do people affected think about the need for, and practicality of preventive measures?

719. What actions can be taken to eliminate or remove risk?

720. What were the Causes that contributed?

721. What can happen?

722. During work activities could hazards exist?

723. How do you handle product safely?

724. Who has a vested interest in how you perform as your organization (our stakeholders)?

725. What are you weak at and therefore need to do better?

726. Are new hazards created?

727. What are your core values?

728. Will revised controls lead to tolerable risk levels?

729. What was measured?

730. How can hazards be reduced?

731. Potential for recurrence?

732. Is the data sufficiently specified in terms of the type of failure being analyzed, and its frequency or probability?

733. What is the chance that it will happen?

2.36 Procurement Management Plan: Maintenance Of Software

734. Are internal Maintenance Of Software project status meetings held at reasonable intervals?

735. Are Maintenance Of Software project team members committed fulltime?

736. Are parking lot items captured?

737. Has a capability assessment been conducted?

738. Why is procurement planning important?

739. Is the Maintenance Of Software project sponsor clearly communicating the business case or rationale for why this Maintenance Of Software project is needed?

740. Are assumptions being identified, recorded, analyzed, qualified and closed?

741. Are stakeholders aware and supportive of the principles and practices of modern software estimation?

742. Have all involved Maintenance Of Software project stakeholders and work groups committed to the Maintenance Of Software project?

743. Are vendor invoices audited for accuracy before payment?

744. Have the procedures for identifying budget variances been followed?

745. Financial capacity; does the seller have, or can the seller reasonably be expected to obtain, the financial resources needed?

746. Are change requests logged and managed?

747. What were things that you did very well and want to do the same again on the next Maintenance Of Software project?

748. Has a sponsor been identified?

749. Is there a set of procedures defining the scope, procedures, and deliverables defining quality control?

750. Does the resource management plan include a personnel development plan?

751. Are procurement deliverables arriving on time and to specification?

752. Is it possible to track all classes of Maintenance Of Software project work (e.g. scheduled, un-scheduled, defect repair, etc.)?

2.37 Source Selection Criteria: Maintenance Of Software

753. How will you decide an evaluators write up is sufficient?

754. Team leads: what is your process for assigning ratings?

755. How are oral presentations documented?

756. Can you prevent comparison of proposals?

757. How long will it take for the purchase cost to be the same as the lease cost?

758. What should be considered?

759. What does an evaluation address and what does a sample resemble?

760. How do you ensure an integrated assessment of proposals?

761. Do you ensure you evaluate what you asked for, not what you want to see or expect to see?

762. What is the last item a Maintenance Of Software project manager must do to finalize Maintenance Of Software project close-out?

763. Who is entitled to a debriefing?

764. What are the most critical evaluation criteria that prove to be tiebreakers in the evaluation of proposals?

765. What source selection software is your team using?

766. What are the steps in performing a cost/tech tradeoff?

767. Can you make a cost/technical tradeoff?

768. Does your documentation identify why the team concurs or differs with reported performance from past performance report (CPARs, questionnaire responses, etc.)?

769. What common questions or problems are associated with debriefings?

770. What should preproposal conferences accomplish?

771. What are the guidelines regarding award without considerations?

772. Is the offeror pricing what is technically proposed?

2.38 Stakeholder Management Plan: Maintenance Of Software

773. Who will be collecting information?

774. Are vendor contract reports, reviews and visits conducted periodically?

775. Are regulatory inspections considered part of quality control?

776. Has a Maintenance Of Software project Communications Plan been developed?

777. Are communication systems currently in place appropriate?

778. Has the schedule been baselined?

779. Has a Maintenance Of Software project Communications Plan been developed?

780. Has a quality assurance plan been developed for the Maintenance Of Software project?

781. How will you engage this stakeholder and gain commitment?

782. If a problem has been detected, what tools can be used to determine a root cause?

783. Contradictory information between different documents?

784. Is the Maintenance Of Software project sponsor clearly communicating the business case or rationale for why this Maintenance Of Software project is needed?

785. Are milestone deliverables effectively tracked and compared to Maintenance Of Software project plan?

786. How are the overall Maintenance Of Software project development processes to be undertaken to produce the Maintenance Of Software project outputs?

787. Is the communication plan being followed?

788. Is there general agreement & acceptance of the current status and progress of the Maintenance Of Software project?

2.39 Change Management Plan: Maintenance Of Software

789. Is there support for this application(s) and are the details available for distribution?

790. Have the business unit contacts been briefed by the Maintenance Of Software project team?

791. Who might be able to help you the most?

792. Has a training need analysis been carried out?

793. What relationships will change?

794. What is going to be done differently?

795. What processes are in place to manage knowledge about the Maintenance Of Software project?

796. Who will do the training?

797. Why is the initiative is being undertaken - What are the business drivers?

798. How might they respond to the message and if the response may be negative or open to misinterpretation, what else needs to be said?

799. Does this change represent a completely new process for your organization, or a different application of an existing process?

800. Who in the business it includes?

801. Have the systems been configured and tested?

802. How will you deal with anger about the restricting of communications due to confidentiality considerations?

803. Are work location changes required?

804. What time commitment will this involve?

805. Readiness -what is a successful end state?

806. Who will be the change levers?

807. Have the business unit contacts been selected and notified?

3.0 Executing Process Group: Maintenance Of Software

808. After how many days will the lease cost be the same as the purchase cost for the equipment?

809. What were things that you did well, and could improve, and how?

810. What are deliverables of your Maintenance Of Software project?

811. What is the product of your Maintenance Of Software project?

812. It under budget or over budget?

813. Have operating capacities been created and/or reinforced in partners?

814. Is the Maintenance Of Software project making progress in helping to achieve the set results?

815. Why do you need a good WBS to use Maintenance Of Software project management software?

816. What are the key components of the Maintenance Of Software project communications plan?

817. How do you prevent staff are just doing busywork to pass the time?

818. Does the case present a realistic scenario?

819. What areas were overlooked on this Maintenance Of Software project?

820. Is the schedule for the set products being met?

821. How well did the chosen processes produce the expected results?

822. In what way has the program come up with innovative measures for problem-solving?

823. What type of information goes in the quality assurance plan?

824. How well did the team follow the chosen processes?

825. Are escalated issues resolved promptly?

826. How do you enter durations, link tasks, and view critical path information?

3.1 Team Member Status Report: Maintenance Of Software

827. Does your organization have the means (staff, money, contract, etc.) to produce or to acquire the product, good, or service?

828. Why is it to be done?

829. Does every department have to have a Maintenance Of Software project Manager on staff?

830. When a teams productivity and success depend on collaboration and the efficient flow of information, what generally fails them?

831. How will resource planning be done?

832. Will the staff do training or is that done by a third party?

833. Do you have an Enterprise Maintenance Of Software project Management Office (EPMO)?

834. How can you make it practical?

835. How it is to be done?

836. Are your organizations Maintenance Of Software projects more successful over time?

837. How does this product, good, or service meet the needs of the Maintenance Of Software project and

your organization as a whole?

838. Are the products of your organizations Maintenance Of Software projects meeting customers objectives?

839. Are the attitudes of staff regarding Maintenance Of Software project work improving?

840. The problem with Reward & Recognition Programs is that the truly deserving people all too often get left out. How can you make it practical?

841. Does the product, good, or service already exist within your organization?

842. How much risk is involved?

843. What specific interest groups do you have in place?

844. Is there evidence that staff is taking a more professional approach toward management of your organizations Maintenance Of Software projects?

845. What is to be done?

3.2 Change Request: Maintenance Of Software

846. How is quality being addressed on the Maintenance Of Software project?

847. Have all related configuration items been properly updated?

848. Can static requirements change attributes like the size of the change be used to predict reliability in execution?

849. How shall the implementation of changes be recorded?

850. What are the requirements for urgent changes?

851. Should a more thorough impact analysis be conducted?

852. How is the change documented (format, content, storage)?

853. How many times must the change be modified or presented to the change control board before it is approved?

854. Are there requirements attributes that are strongly related to the complexity and size?

855. Can you answer what happened, who did it, when did it happen, and what else will be affected?

856. When to submit a change request?

857. Why were your requested changes rejected or not made?

858. How do you get changes (code) out in a timely manner?

859. What is the purpose of change control?

860. Will new change requests be acknowledged in a timely manner?

861. How are changes graded and who is responsible for the rating?

862. Are there requirements attributes that can discriminate between high and low reliability?

863. What is the function of the change control committee?

864. Who will perform the change?

3.3 Change Log: Maintenance Of Software

865. Who initiated the change request?

866. How does this change affect scope?

867. Where do changes come from?

868. How does this change affect the timeline of the schedule?

869. Is the requested change request a result of changes in other Maintenance Of Software project(s)?

870. When was the request submitted?

871. When was the request approved?

872. Is the change backward compatible without limitations?

873. Do the described changes impact on the integrity or security of the system?

874. Will the Maintenance Of Software project fail if the change request is not executed?

875. Is the change request open, closed or pending?

876. Is the change request within Maintenance Of Software project scope?

877. Is the submitted change a new change or a modification of a previously approved change?

878. How does this relate to the standards developed for specific business processes?

879. Does the suggested change request represent a desired enhancement to the products functionality?

880. Is this a mandatory replacement?

3.4 Decision Log: Maintenance Of Software

881. Decision-making process; how will the team make decisions?

882. At what point in time does loss become unacceptable?

883. How does the use a Decision Support System influence the strategies/tactics or costs?

884. What is the average size of your matters in an applicable measurement?

885. Meeting purpose; why does this team meet?

886. How effective is maintaining the log at facilitating organizational learning?

887. What is the line where eDiscovery ends and document review begins?

888. Do strategies and tactics aimed at less than full control reduce the costs of management or simply shift the cost burden?

889. Adversarial environment. is your opponent open to a non-traditional workflow, or will it likely challenge anything you do?

890. Does anything need to be adjusted?

891. Which variables make a critical difference?

892. What are the cost implications?

893. What was the rationale for the decision?

894. Linked to original objective?

895. What makes you different or better than others companies selling the same thing?

896. What eDiscovery problem or issue did your organization set out to fix or make better?

897. How consolidated and comprehensive a story can you tell by capturing currently available incident data in a central location and through a log of key decisions during an incident?

898. Behaviors; what are guidelines that the team has identified that will assist them with getting the most out of team meetings?

899. How do you define success?

900. With whom was the decision shared or considered?

3.5 Quality Audit: Maintenance Of Software

901. How does your organization know that the range and quality of its accommodation, catering and transportation services are appropriately effective and constructive?

902. What is the collective experience of the team to be assigned to an audit?

903. How does your organization know that the review processes are effective?

904. Are the policies and processes, as set out in the Quality Audit Manual, properly applied?

905. How does your organization know that its staff have appropriate access to a fair and effective grievance process?

906. Is there a written corporate quality policy?

907. What does the organizarion look for in a Quality audit?

908. What are your supplier audits?

909. Are salvageable and salvaged medical devices stored in a manner to prevent damage and/or contamination?

910. How does your organization know that its

relationships with industry and employers are appropriately effective and constructive?

911. Health and safety arrangements; stress management workshops. How does your organization know that it provides a safe and healthy environment?

912. Are all staff empowered and encouraged to contribute to ongoing improvement efforts?

913. What does an analysis of your organizations staff profile suggest in terms of its planning, and how is this being addressed?

914. What review processes are in place for your organizations major activities?

915. How does your organization know that it provides a safe and healthy environment?

916. Does the audit organization have experience in performing the required work for entities of your type and size?

917. What experience do staff have in the type of work that the audit entails?

918. Does the report read coherently?

919. Is your organizations resource allocation system properly aligned with its collection of intentions?

920. Are multiple statements on the same issue consistent with each other?

3.6 Team Directory: Maintenance Of Software

921. Who will write the meeting minutes and distribute?

922. What needs to be communicated?

923. Process decisions: is work progressing on schedule and per contract requirements?

924. Who should receive information (all stakeholders)?

925. Is construction on schedule?

926. Decisions: is the most suitable form of contract being used?

927. Process decisions: which organizational elements and which individuals will be assigned management functions?

928. Who are the Team Members?

929. Who will be the stakeholders on your next Maintenance Of Software project?

930. Contract requirements complied with?

931. Have you decided when to celebrate the Maintenance Of Software projects completion date?

932. Who will talk to the customer?

933. How will the team handle changes?

934. Process decisions: how well was task order work performed?

935. Process decisions: are all start-up, turn over and close out requirements of the contract satisfied?

936. Decisions: what could be done better to improve the quality of the constructed product?

937. When does information need to be distributed?

938. What are you going to deliver or accomplish?

939. Process decisions: are contractors adequately prosecuting the work?

3.7 Team Operating Agreement: Maintenance Of Software

940. Reimbursements: how will the team members be reimbursed for expenses and time commitments?

941. Do you post any action items, due dates, and responsibilities on the team website?

942. Do you listen for voice tone and word choice to understand the meaning behind words?

943. What is teaming?

944. How will group handle unplanned absences?

945. Have you established procedures that team members can follow to work effectively together, such as a team operating agreement?

946. How will you resolve conflict efficiently and respectfully?

947. Do you solicit member feedback about meetings and what would make them better?

948. Is compensation based on team and individual performance?

949. Do you ensure that all participants know how to use the required technology?

950. Are there the right people on your team?

951. To whom do you deliver your services?

952. How does teaming fit in with overall organizational goals and meet organizational needs?

953. What is group supervision?

954. Are there more than two native languages represented by your team?

955. Do you record meetings for the already stated unable to attend?

956. What resources can be provided for the team in terms of equipment, space, time for training, protected time and space for meetings, and travel allowances?

957. Do you call or email participants to ensure understanding, follow-through and commitment to the meeting outcomes?

958. The method to be used in the decision making process; Will it be consensus, majority rule, or the supervisor having the final say?

959. Confidentiality: how will confidential information be handled?

3.8 Team Performance Assessment: Maintenance Of Software

960. To what degree can the team ensure that all members are individually and jointly accountable for the teams purpose, goals, approach, and work-products?

961. To what degree will the team adopt a concrete, clearly understood, and agreed-upon approach that will result in achievement of the teams goals?

962. To what degree will team members, individually and collectively, commit time to help themselves and others learn and develop skills?

963. To what degree can team members frequently and easily communicate with one another?

964. To what degree can all members engage in open and interactive considerations?

965. To what degree are the relative importance and priority of the goals clear to all team members?

966. To what degree are the skill areas critical to team performance present?

967. What are teams?

968. To what degree does the team possess adequate membership to achieve its ends?

969. To what degree can team members vigorously define the teams purpose in considerations with others who are not part of the functioning team?

970. What is method variance?

971. Do you give group members authority to make at least some important decisions?

972. To what degree does the teams purpose contain themes that are particularly meaningful and memorable?

973. Do friends perform better than acquaintances?

974. Do you promptly inform members about major developments that may affect them?

975. To what degree do the goals specify concrete team work products?

976. Delaying market entry: how long is too long?

977. To what degree does the teams approach to its work allow for modification and improvement over time?

978. To what degree do team members agree with the goals, relative importance, and the ways in which achievement will be measured?

3.9 Team Member Performance Assessment: Maintenance Of Software

979. How effective is training that is delivered through technology-based platforms?

980. To what degree do team members articulate the teams work approach?

981. What are best practices for delivering and developing training evaluations to maximize the benefits of leveraging emerging technologies?

982. Why do performance reviews?

983. Does adaptive training work?

984. Where can team members go for more detailed information on performance measurement and assessment?

985. Are any validation activities performed?

986. How often are assessments to be conducted?

987. Is there reluctance to join a team?

988. To what degree is the team cognizant of small wins to be celebrated along the way?

989. What are they responsible for?

990. Should a ratee get a copy of all the raters documents about the employees performance?

991. How do you currently use the time that is available?

992. How accurately is your plan implemented?

993. How will they be formed?

994. How do you use data to inform instruction and improve staff achievement?

995. How are training activities developed from a technical perspective?

996. To what degree is there a sense that only the team can succeed?

997. What evaluation results did you have?

998. What are the key duties or tasks of the Ratee?

3.10 Issue Log: Maintenance Of Software

999. What is the impact on the risks?

1000. What is a Stakeholder?

1001. What are the stakeholders interrelationships?

1002. How do you manage communications?

1003. Who is the issue assigned to?

1004. Are the stakeholders getting the information they need, are they consulted, are concerns addressed?

1005. What date was the issue resolved?

1006. Is access to the Issue Log controlled?

1007. Why not more evaluators?

1008. Why do you manage communications?

1009. How were past initiatives successful?

1010. In classifying stakeholders, which approach to do so are you using?

1011. Can an impact cause deviation beyond team, stage or Maintenance Of Software project tolerances?

1012. Do you feel a register helps?

1013. What help do you and your team need from the stakeholders?

1014. How much time does it take to do it?

1015. Do you have members of your team responsible for certain stakeholders?

4.0 Monitoring and Controlling Process Group: Maintenance Of Software

1016. Does the solution fit in with organizations technical architectural requirements?

1017. Are the necessary foundations in place to ensure the sustainability of the results of the programme?

1018. How many potential communications channels exist on the Maintenance Of Software project?

1019. Did it work?

1020. How many more potential communications channels were introduced by the discovery of the new stakeholders?

1021. Is the program making progress in helping to achieve the set results?

1022. Is progress on outcomes due to your program?

1023. What resources are necessary?

1024. Based on your Maintenance Of Software project communication management plan, what worked well?

1025. How do you monitor progress?

1026. Change, where should you look for problems?

1027. How is Agile Maintenance Of Software project Management done?

1028. How was the program set-up initiated?

1029. Accuracy: what design will lead to accurate information?

1030. Are there areas that need improvement?

1031. Is there sufficient time allotted between the general system design and the detailed system design phases?

1032. Purpose: toward what end is the evaluation being conducted?

4.1 Project Performance Report: Maintenance Of Software

1033. To what degree will each member have the opportunity to advance his or her professional skills in all three of the above categories while contributing to the accomplishment of the teams purpose and goals?

1034. To what degree are the goals realistic?

1035. To what degree are the demands of the task compatible with and converge with the relationships of the informal organization?

1036. To what degree does the task meet individual needs?

1037. To what degree do members articulate the goals beyond the team membership?

1038. To what degree will the team ensure that all members equitably share the work essential to the success of the team?

1039. To what degree do team members feel that the purpose of the team is important, if not exciting?

1040. To what degree are the members clear on what they are individually responsible for and what they are jointly responsible for?

1041. To what degree do the relationships of the informal organization motivate taskrelevant behavior and facilitate task completion?

1042. To what degree does the teams work approach provide opportunity for members to engage in open interaction?

1043. What is the degree to which rules govern information exchange between individuals within your organization?

1044. What degree are the relative importance and priority of the goals clear to all team members?

4.2 Variance Analysis: Maintenance Of Software

1045. Are data elements reconcilable between internal summary reports and reports forwarded to the stakeholders?

1046. Are records maintained to show how undistributed budgets are controlled?

1047. What was the cause of the increase in costs?

1048. How do you verify authorization to proceed with all authorized work?

1049. What are the actual costs to date?

1050. Is the anticipated (firm and potential) business base Maintenance Of Software projected in a rational, consistent manner?

1051. How are material, labor, and overhead standards set?

1052. Other relevant issues of Variance Analysis -selling price or gross margin?

1053. Can process improvements lead to unfavorable variances?

1054. Does the accounting system provide a basis for auditing records of direct costs chargeable to the contract?

1055. Are detailed work packages planned as far in advance as practicable?

1056. Did your organization lose existing customers and/or gain new customers?

1057. How do you identify potential or actual overruns and underruns?

1058. Are your organizations and items of cost assigned to each pool identified?

1059. What can be the cause of an increase in costs?

1060. Why are standard cost systems used?

1061. Are records maintained to show how management reserves are used?

1062. Is all contract work included in the CWBS?

1063. What should management do?

4.3 Earned Value Status: Maintenance Of Software

1064. Are you hitting your Maintenance Of Software projects targets?

1065. Verification is a process of ensuring that the developed system satisfies the stakeholders agreements and specifications; Are you building the product right? What do you verify?

1066. Where is evidence-based earned value in your organization reported?

1067. How much is it going to cost by the finish?

1068. If earned value management (EVM) is so good in determining the true status of a Maintenance Of Software project and Maintenance Of Software project its completion, why is it that hardly any one uses it in information systems related Maintenance Of Software projects?

1069. Validation is a process of ensuring that the developed system will actually achieve the stakeholders desired outcomes; Are you building the right product? What do you validate?

1070. What is the unit of forecast value?

1071. How does this compare with other Maintenance Of Software projects?

1072. Earned value can be used in almost any
Maintenance Of Software project situation and
in almost any Maintenance Of Software project
environment. it may be used on large Maintenance
Of Software projects, medium sized Maintenance
Of Software projects, tiny Maintenance Of Software
projects (in cut-down form), complex and simple
Maintenance Of Software projects and in any market
sector. some people, of course, know all about earned
value, they have used it for years - but perhaps not as
effectively as they could have?

1073. When is it going to finish?

1074. Where are your problem areas?

4.4 Risk Audit: Maintenance Of Software

1075. Are procedures developed to respond to foreseeable emergencies and communicated to all involved?

1076. How effective are your risk controls?

1077. What is the effect of globalisation; is business becoming too complex and can the auditor rely on auditing standards?

1078. What risk does not having unique identification present?

1079. To what extent are auditors influenced by the business risk assessment in the audit process, and how can auditors create more effective mental models to more fully examine contradictory evidence?

1080. What expertise does the Board have on quality, outcomes, and errors?

1081. Is the technology to be built new to your organization?

1082. What are the differences and similarities between strategic and operational risks in your organization?

1083. Are end-users enthusiastically committed to

the Maintenance Of Software project and the system/ product to be built?

1084. Are all managers or operators of the facility or equipment competent or qualified?

1085. Is Maintenance Of Software project scope stable?

1086. Is safety information provided to all involved?

1087. Where will the next scandal or adverse media involving your organization come from?

1088. How will you maximise opportunities?

1089. What is the Board doing to assure measurement and improve outcomes and quality and reduce avoidable adverse events?

1090. What does internal control mean in the context of the audit process?

1091. Are some people working on multiple Maintenance Of Software projects?

1092. Does your organization have an up-to-date constitution?

1093. Do you have an understanding of insurance claims processes?

1094. Are regular safety inspections made of buildings, grounds and equipment?

4.5 Contractor Status Report: Maintenance Of Software

1095. What process manages the contracts?

1096. What is the average response time for answering a support call?

1097. If applicable; describe your standard schedule for new software version releases. Are new software version releases included in the standard maintenance plan?

1098. Describe how often regular updates are made to the proposed solution. Are corresponding regular updates included in the standard maintenance plan?

1099. What are the minimum and optimal bandwidth requirements for the proposed solution?

1100. What was the overall budget or estimated cost?

1101. How does the proposed individual meet each requirement?

1102. What was the budget or estimated cost for your organizations services?

1103. Who can list a Maintenance Of Software project as organization experience, your organization or a previous employee of your organization?

1104. What was the actual budget or estimated cost

for your organizations services?

1105. How long have you been using the services?

1106. What was the final actual cost?

1107. Are there contractual transfer concerns?

1108. How is risk transferred?

4.6 Formal Acceptance: Maintenance Of Software

1109. Do you buy pre-configured systems or build your own configuration?

1110. What are the requirements against which to test, Who will execute?

1111. Does it do what Maintenance Of Software project team said it would?

1112. Do you buy-in installation services?

1113. What function(s) does it fill or meet?

1114. Was the Maintenance Of Software project goal achieved?

1115. How does your team plan to obtain formal acceptance on your Maintenance Of Software project?

1116. General estimate of the costs and times to complete the Maintenance Of Software project?

1117. Was the Maintenance Of Software project work done on time, within budget, and according to specification?

1118. Does it do what client said it would?

1119. What features, practices, and processes proved to be strengths or weaknesses?

1120. What can you do better next time?

1121. Was the Maintenance Of Software project managed well?

1122. Did the Maintenance Of Software project achieve its MOV?

1123. Was the sponsor/customer satisfied?

1124. Who would use it?

1125. Do you perform formal acceptance or burn-in tests?

1126. Who supplies data?

1127. Did the Maintenance Of Software project manager and team act in a professional and ethical manner?

1128. Have all comments been addressed?

5.0 Closing Process Group: Maintenance Of Software

1129. Were the outcomes different from the already stated planned?

1130. Is this a follow-on to a previous Maintenance Of Software project?

1131. Did the Maintenance Of Software project team have enough people to execute the Maintenance Of Software project plan?

1132. How well defined and documented were the Maintenance Of Software project management processes you chose to use?

1133. What could have been improved?

1134. What do you need to do?

1135. If action is called for, what form should it take?

1136. How will you know you did it?

1137. What is the risk of failure to your organization?

1138. Did you do what you said you were going to do?

1139. What were the actual outcomes?

1140. What communication items need improvement?

1141. How well did the chosen processes fit the needs of the Maintenance Of Software project?

1142. What could be done to improve the process?

1143. Was the user/client satisfied with the end product?

1144. How well did you do?

1145. Did you do things well?

1146. Is the Maintenance Of Software project funded?

1147. Does the close educate others to improve performance?

5.1 Procurement Audit: Maintenance Of Software

1148. Are procurement processes well organized and documented?

1149. Does your organization have a purchasing policy ?

1150. Was the suitability of candidates accurately assessed?

1151. Has guidelines been set up for how the procurement function/unit should carry out its procurements?

1152. Was invitation to tender to each specific contract issued after the evaluation of the indicative tenders was completed?

1153. Which are the main risks and controls of each phase?

1154. Does the strategy contain incentives to evaluate the performance of the procurement function/unit?

1155. Are criteria and sub-criteria set suitable to identify the tender that offers best value for money?

1156. Was the award criteria that of the most economically advantageous tender?

1157. Is electronic procurement applied to reduce

transaction costs?

1158. Budget controls: does your organization maintain an up-to-date (approved) budget for all funded activities, and perform a comparison of that budget with actual expenditures for each budget category?

1159. Does the strategy ensure that appropriate controls are in place to ensure propriety and regularity in delivery?

1160. Did the contracting authority offer unrestricted and full electronic access to the contract documents and any supplementary documents (specifying the internet address in the notice)?

1161. If information was withheld, was there reasonable justification for this decision?

1162. Is there a legal authority for the procurement Maintenance Of Software project?

1163. Were products/services not received within the prescribed time limit?

1164. Is a risk evaluation performed?

1165. Is there a need for the procurement Maintenance Of Software project at all?

1166. Are there performance targets on value for money obtained and cost savings?

1167. If an order is divided among several vendors, is the explanation for that procedure documented?

5.2 Contract Close-Out: Maintenance Of Software

1168. What happens to the recipient of services?

1169. Have all contracts been closed?

1170. Change in knowledge?

1171. Are the signers the authorized officials?

1172. How/when used ?

1173. How is the contracting office notified of the automatic contract close-out?

1174. Why Outsource?

1175. Have all contract records been included in the Maintenance Of Software project archives?

1176. Change in attitude or behavior?

1177. How does it work?

1178. Have all contracts been completed?

1179. What is capture management?

1180. Have all acceptance criteria been met prior to final payment to contractors?

1181. Parties: who is involved?

1182. Parties: Authorized?

1183. Has each contract been audited to verify acceptance and delivery?

1184. Change in circumstances?

1185. Was the contract sufficiently clear so as not to result in numerous disputes and misunderstandings?

1186. Was the contract type appropriate?

1187. Was the contract complete without requiring numerous changes and revisions?

5.3 Project or Phase Close-Out: Maintenance Of Software

1188. Was the schedule met?

1189. What were the goals and objectives of the communications strategy for the Maintenance Of Software project?

1190. Planned completion date?

1191. How much influence did the stakeholder have over others?

1192. Which changes might a stakeholder be required to make as a result of the Maintenance Of Software project?

1193. In preparing the Lessons Learned report, should it reflect a consensus viewpoint, or should the report reflect the different individual viewpoints?

1194. Planned remaining costs?

1195. Complete yes or no?

1196. What benefits or impacts does the stakeholder group expect to obtain as a result of the Maintenance Of Software project?

1197. What are the marketing communication needs for each stakeholder?

1198. What is a Risk?

1199. Who exerted influence that has positively affected or negatively impacted the Maintenance Of Software project?

1200. Is the lesson based on actual Maintenance Of Software project experience rather than on independent research?

1201. Did the delivered product meet the specified requirements and goals of the Maintenance Of Software project?

1202. What was learned?

1203. Can the lesson learned be replicated?

1204. Is there a clear cause and effect between the activity and the lesson learned?

1205. What hierarchical authority does the stakeholder have in your organization?

5.4 Lessons Learned: Maintenance Of Software

1206. How effective was the documentation that you received with the Maintenance Of Software project product/service?

1207. How well defined were the acceptance criteria for Maintenance Of Software project deliverables?

1208. How smooth do you feel Integration has been?

1209. How well do you feel the executives supported this Maintenance Of Software project?

1210. What skills are required for the task?

1211. What is the fiscal dependency?

1212. What is the supervisor to staff ratio?

1213. Was sufficient time allocated to review Maintenance Of Software project deliverables?

1214. How does the budget cycle affect the case?

1215. How satisfied are you with your involvement in the development and/or review of the Maintenance Of Software project Scope during Maintenance Of Software project Initiation and Planning?

1216. Is the lesson based on actual Maintenance Of Software project experience rather than on independent research?

1217. What were the major enablers to a quick response?

1218. What were the challenges and pitfalls?

1219. How effectively were issues resolved before escalation was necessary?

1220. Is the lesson significant, valid, and applicable?

1221. How well were your expectations met regarding the extent of your involvement in the Maintenance Of Software project (effort, time commitments, etc.)?

1222. How efficient were Maintenance Of Software project team meetings conducted?

1223. What is the expected lifespan of the deliverable?

1224. How effectively were issues managed on the Maintenance Of Software project?

Index

270

277

Printed in Great Britain
by Amazon

82416779R00176